TINY BUDDHA'S 365 *Tiny Love Challenges*

LORI DESCHENE

 For information address HarperCollins Publishers, 195 Broadway, New York, NY 10007.

HarperCollins books may be purchased for educational, business, or sales promotional use. For information please e-mail the Special Markets Department at SPsales@harpercollins.com.

HarperCollins website: http://www.harpercollins.com

First Edition

Designed by Howie Severson

Library of Congress Cataloging-in-Publication Data is available upon request.

ISBN 978–0–06–238585–7

15 16 17 18 19 RRD(H) 10 9 8 7 6 5 4 3 2 1

For Ehren;
Home is where you are.
And for the family night crew;
I love every loud dinner I get to share with you!

Contents

Introduction

It's ironic, isn't it? We live in a world with billions of people, and we're more connected than ever through our rapidly advancing technology, yet many of us feel disconnected—if not physically, then emotionally.

We collect friends online like pennies in a jar, and in much the same way, it doesn't always feel all that valuable. Sure, you might get a "like" here and there, and you may even command more than your share of comments on updates about your breakfast, your birthday, or your baby. To be fair, you may also have incredibly deep and meaningful connections, online and off, and you may have bought this book to strengthen them even further. But many of us find ourselves with an ever-growing friend list that doesn't necessarily translate to an increased sense of belonging or closeness.

We all need to feel not just connected but deeply seen and accepted. We need to feel that people get us, value us, and love us—flaws and all. To meet these needs—and meet them for others—we have to open up, step outside ourselves, and prioritize our relationships. But we don't always do these things, perhaps because we get caught up pursuing everything that seems to be missing from our lives; or, if you're like I was, you may not have fulfilling relationships because you don't yet believe you're worthy of them.

For much of my life, I focused all my energy on improving myself and my circumstances because I thought others would only see my value if I became someone better. It was only after years of pushing myself—and ostracizing myself, in fear of being seen and judged as inadequate—that I realized yet another irony: I didn't need to be someone else or somewhere else to get what I wanted; I needed to accept who I was and be right where I was. Because right there, in the present, there were loved ones I failed to acknowledge while wrapped up in my self-involvement, there were friends I'd yet to meet, and wouldn't, if I didn't get out of my head and look around, and there was a whole lot of love I could be giving if only I stopped worrying about the love I wasn't getting.

If you've ever visited tinybuddha.com, the website I started in 2009, you may have recognized in reading the blog and forum posts that we're all more similar than we are different. Every one of us wants to find our place in the world and feel part of something larger than ourselves. Every one of us wants to feel that other people care and will be there for us. Every one of us wants to form and maintain close, loving relationships. And every last one of us can do something, no matter how small, to create these relationships right now.

The challenges in this book are all things I've worked at since deciding to focus less on myself and more on the people around me. While I'd like to say I make time every day for a thoughtful conversation, a kind gesture, or even just a few moments of reflection, I sometimes struggle with consistency. If I'm not deliberate, I can easily fall back into old habits of self-absorption and get bogged down by worries, wants, and obligations. On those days, I try to remember not only how much better I feel when I prioritize loving others in action, but also how much better the world would be if we all did this more often. That's why I created this book: to help us all remember to do something, every day, to make the world a kinder, more loving place.

Though the majority of the challenges here involve other people, many pertain to self-love, since we need to love ourselves before we can truly love or be loved by someone else. They're all simple, but that doesn't mean they're easy. Some might test you, stretch you, and draw your attention to fears and beliefs you've never before acknowledged.

Some might surprise you in their difficulty, given how simple they look on paper. Others may be things you already do regularly, and with ease.

Regardless of how challenging these are for you, if you commit to working on these things daily, you will slowly start to see benefits. The challenges may help you:

- Develop closer bonds in your relationships
- Let your guard down more easily to let people in
- Express your feelings instead of hiding them
- Let go of anger, bitterness, and fear
- See the best in the people around you
- Relate to and better understand your loved ones
- Let go of insecurity so you can relax in your interactions
- Turn strangers into friends
- Attract healthier relationships—and believe that you deserve them

I've organized the challenges by month with eleven different themes, as outlined in the table of contents. As you likely noticed, "Kindness and Thoughtfulness" starts the book and makes a comeback at the midpoint. Since all loving relationships grow from a foundation of thoughtfulness—and because acts of kindness can be both fun and rewarding—it seemed fitting to start both the first and second half of the year with this theme. My hope is that by working on each of these areas for an entire month, at the end you'll find it easier, if not instinctive, to regularly practice these habits.

At the start of each week, you'll find one or two relevant stories from Tiny Buddha contributors, who've shared their experiences, insights, and lessons on giving and receiving love. If you'd like to learn more about any of these individuals, flip to the back of the book to find more information about them in the contributor index. I've included two of my own stories in July and September. For consistency, and to avoid confusion, I've put my name on top of these.

Almost every challenge page includes questions for reflection, which may help you complete the activity or put you in the right headspace to do it, and space on the bottom to write about your experience at the end of the day. You may want to get a separate notebook if you'd like more room for writing. (Even if you choose not to track your daily progress, you may want to keep a pen nearby, as some of the challenges involve short writing exercises.) Alternatively—or in addition—you're welcome to visit the forum at http://tinybuddha.com/love-forums to share your experiences with other readers. Although I've arranged the challenges by theme, you don't have work through the book from start to finish. If you prefer, you could do one week on a given theme and then pick a different theme the following week; or, you could open to any page when you wake up in the morning and do whichever challenge you see. You'll notice the final week of every month includes more than seven challenges. This is to accommodate for the additional two to three days in a given month.

However you choose to use the book, I hope it helps you feel more loving, more lovable, and more loved. And I hope it helps you feel more connected—to yourself, to the people around you, and to the world at large—one tiny action at a time.

JANUARY

Kindness and Thoughtfulness

Reflections from ERNEST DEMPSEY

Maybe you've experienced it before—that feeling of dread when you're driving down the highway and suddenly something goes wrong. You're stepping on the gas pedal but nothing is happening. All the little lights on the dashboard come on, and you notice one particular gauge you've been meaning to address sooner. The needle is just past the E. You're out of gas.

Desperation flashes through your mind as the wheels begin to slow. Other cars start passing you as you attempt to merge over to the emergency lane to get out of the way, the whole time hoping you can coast just a little farther, ever closer to the oasis of fuel at the next exit.

I experienced this recently when I was cruising down a long hill on the interstate and ran out of gas. Fortunately, I was able to get over and coast all the way to the next exit and even up the ramp. When my vehicle's momentum finally slowed to a stop, I was relieved to see the gas station only a few hundred yards away, and that I'd only have to overcome a slight incline to get there.

So I got out and started pushing. As I grunted and heaved, I was unpleasantly surprised at how heavy my little car was on a relatively flat stretch of road. My muscles strained against the heavy burden, legs and arms burning from the exertion. Suddenly, the car felt like it was half its weight. I first looked down to see if I'd reached some kind of a downslope. Then I heard a guy's voice from behind me.

"Thought you could use a little help."

I turned around to see a total stranger pushing hard against the back end of my car. I smiled broadly.

"Thanks, man!" I shouted over the passing traffic.

He had parked his truck just off the exit, probably as soon as he had seen my plight. He hadn't hesitated or thought about helping me for more than a second.

"You should be okay once we get to that little downslope up ahead," he commented.

A minute or so later, we reached the downhill section of road and my car began coast. "I think you're good," he yelled and waved.

I thanked the man again and hopped in my car, steering it into the station on nothing but gravity's sweet momentum. I don't know much about karma, but I do know this: life presents us with opportunities, little moments where we can make the world a better place with a simple action. That stranger made my day better by lending a hand, a simple action that lightened my load and thus lifted my spirits. Had he not helped, I may have become annoyed at the situation and more easily bothered the rest of the day. I could have returned home less happy and let those feelings pass from me to the people around me, making their day worse.

We have an extraordinary power to change someone's day for better or worse, and we have no idea how far-reaching that impact will be.

I kept smiling as I filled up my tank, feeling grateful that a random stranger had helped me. As I started to replace the gas cap, I heard a familiar sound on the other side of the pump. A police officer in an old, beat-up pickup truck was trying in vain to get the engine to turn over.

"Battery dead?" I asked. "If you need a jump, I have some jumper cables in the trunk," I offered. The man's frustration visibly eased a little.

"Thanks, man," he replied. "I'd appreciate that."

"No problem," I said as I reached in the trunk and grabbed the cables. "It's always good to help someone out."

JANUARY 1

Challenge

Help a stranger in need.

Brainstorm: *Give someone coins for a parking meter, open a door for a mother pushing a stroller, or offer to help someone who's carrying something that looks heavy.*

For Reflection

When was the last time you saw a stranger in need of help? Did you stop to assist, and if not, why?

What, if anything, has prevented you from helping strangers in the past, and how can you overcome this?

Has a stranger ever offered assistance to you, and how and why was this helpful?

How Did It Go?

Who did you help, and how do you think it made a positive difference in that person's day?

JANUARY 2

Challenge

Ask your newest friends or coworkers when their birthdays are so you can make a note of this for the future. Then be sure to wish them a happy birthday!

Tip: *Immediately put the birthdays in your calendar—whether digital or physical—and schedule an alert, if possible, so that you remember when it rolls around.*

For Reflection

Who are some new people in your life with whom you'd like to develop closer relationships?

What's something simple you can plan to do for these people to honor their birthdays? (Write on their Facebook walls? Send cards in the mail? Send e-cards?)

How Did It Go?

Whose birthday is coming up soon? Could you start planning something now?

JANUARY 3

Challenge

Ask a friend or coworker who seems frazzled
if you can help with anything.

For Reflection

How do you usually look or act when you're frazzled and in need of help?

How does it affect your life and your relationships when you feel overwhelmed?

What's the most helpful thing someone could say or do for you when you're feeling this way?

How Did It Go?

Did your friend or coworker accept your offer? If so, what did you do to help?

JANUARY 4

Challenge

Focus on one thing at a time today instead of multitasking, as an act of kindness to your overworked brain.

For Reflection

How do you feel when you try to accomplish many things at once?

What unkind things do you say to yourself when you struggle to do this effectively?

What can you say to yourself that would be kinder when you're tempted to do too much?

How Did It Go?

How did it affect your state of mind—and your day—to focus on one thing at a time?

JANUARY 5

Challenge

Connect two friends or acquaintances that you believe could help each other, or who might hit it off romantically.

For Reflection

Has a friend or coworker ever made an introduction for you that changed your life? If so, how did this affect your life for the better?

What might have happened (or might not have happened) if not for this introduction?

How Did It Go?

Were the people you introduced excited to connect with each other?

JANUARY 6

Challenge

Carry with you one thing that someone else may need so that you can help them out should the opportunity arise.

Brainstorm: *You could carry a pen, an aspirin, a safety pin, a paper clip, or a Tide pen.*

For Reflection

What type of things do you often need throughout the day? Do you have any of these items in your home?

Has someone ever offered you something they had on hand that helped you out? Why did you appreciate this?

How Did It Go?

Did you have an opportunity to offer the item you carried with you? If so, how was this helpful to the other person?

JANUARY 7

Challenge

Write down one to three choices that often compromise your ability to be kind, and for each, one proactive thing you can do today to address that issue.

Brainstorm: *For example, if you're less kind when you're hungry, eat breakfast instead of having just coffee, or, if you're less kind when you feel stressed, take a walk in nature after work to clear your head.*

1. Choice that compromises your ability to be kind:

   One proactive thing you can do to address this:

2. Choice that compromises your ability to be kind:

   One proactive thing you can do to address this:

3. Choice that compromises your ability to be kind:

   One proactive thing you can do to address this:

How Did It Go?

If you put into practice one or more of your proactive ideas, how did these small changes affect your demeanor—and your interactions?

A few years ago, a lady in her midforties brushed past me in the grocery store, knocking over my basket and causing its contents to spill about. I was livid, as I was having a particularly bad day, so I let out an exasperated profanity (or two) and bent over to start picking things up. "I'm sorry," she said, "I'm just having the worst day."

I looked up, ready to rip her a new one, but my anger was diffused almost immediately when I saw the look on her face. I'd seen it in my own reflection so many times—pure defeat. Making light of the situation, I said, "It's okay; I'll just tell them the eggs were already broken." She laughed and offered to pay for my groceries, and we ended up having coffee together at the Coffee Bean inside the store.

She told me she had just been diagnosed with stage 4 breast cancer—something I would've never known had I stormed off in anger.

"You have my full permission to knock over anyone you want coming through that door," I said, and she smiled.

This one encounter is the reason I no longer get angry when someone bumps into me, or cuts me off in traffic, and it's also probably why I am so intrigued by strangers. No one carries a sign around on their back advertising their problems. So I can't ever know what someone's life is like unless they tell me. But if an act of kindness has the ability to shift someone's bad day into a better one, then why not try to be that change?

Everyone has a battle that they're fighting, and as people who occupy the same traveling spaces we should try to treat each other like neighbors—because for that moment while we're standing next to each other, that's exactly what we are.

I am not, by nature, a kind person. But I'm trying to be. I'm far too often the first to come back with a sharp retort. Sarcasm and I were old companions, until about four years ago, when I had what I thought was just a casual conversation with a friend. But the next time I saw her, there was a distance between us. I finally had a chance to speak with her alone and ask what was the matter.

"You always have to get a shot in," she responded.

Oh. I couldn't even remember what we'd been talking about. Nothing important, really. I *did* know I hadn't meant to be cruel. That whatever it was I'd said, I'd only meant it as teasing. A chance to be clever, witty. But I've learned that it's better to be kind than clever. That too often what I think is witty is closer to hurtful. I may think we're playing, trading silly jests, but I don't know how the other person is feeling that day. Something that may normally ride lightly on them may strike an unknown injury and remind them of another hurt.

I don't want to be, or be known as, the person who always gets a shot in; the person my friends are hesitant to chat with, because they don't know if they're going to be next to be teased. So I'm willing to work at nurturing kindness and thinking before I speak. Taking a sip of water or a bite of my sandwich creates space to think about my reply, and often reshape it, soften it, or discard it all together. When I realize I've already said something harsh, or something that could be interpreted as harsh, I apologize immediately because I'd rather not risk being misunderstood.

I can feel myself softening, becoming a gentler person. My sharp edges seem to be smoothing away. Not all the way down, but enough that kindness doesn't feel like a foreign language to my tongue. Someday, I might even think of it as second nature. And when kindness comes naturally, we're being kind to ourselves and others.

JANUARY 8

Challenge

Today, when someone does something that annoys or inconveniences you, choose to cut them slack instead of giving them a hard time.

Brainstorm: *Be forgiving when someone cuts you off in traffic, or be patient when your waiter gets your order wrong.*

For Reflection

Do you often feel the need to let people know when they've annoyed or inconvenienced you—and if yes, why?

What does this accomplish?

What would you need to tell yourself to be able to let it go instead?

How Did It Go?

What helped you challenge your knee-jerk reaction so that you could respond differently?

JANUARY 9

Challenge

Do one small task to make someone's life easier.

Brainstorm: *Wash the dishes so your spouse won't have to, offer to pick up your roommate's prescription at the pharmacy, or bring a tired, hardworking coworker a coffee.*

For Reflection

When was the last time someone did something little to make your life easier?

Would it have occurred to you to ask someone to do this for you?

Do you usually look for ways to make life easier for others? If not, why? What obstacles get in the way, and how can you overcome those?

How Did It Go?

Who did you help, and why was this small thing actually a big thing?

JANUARY 10

Challenge

Write down three things you hope people do and three things you hope they *don't* do when speaking to your child (or future child). Remember these things today when you're speaking to others to help you be kinder.

Brainstorm: *DO listen fully, be patient;*
DON'T interrupt, get defensive.

DO

1.
2.
3.

DON'T

1.
2.
3.

How Did It Go?

Did you stop yourself before speaking unkindly to someone today as a result of this exercise? How did you feel, and how did this affect the conversation?

JANUARY 11

Challenge

Tell someone about an act of kindness you recently witnessed, to lift both of your spirits and to potentially inspire future acts of kindness.

For Reflection

Why did this particular act of kindness warm your heart or renew your faith in people?

Did witnessing this change your day for the better?

How might it affect all of us for the better if we focused more on positive stories, like this, and less on negative stories that only bring us down?

How Did It Go?

Who did you share this with, and how did they respond? Did sharing this story affect you in a positive way?

JANUARY 12

Challenge

Let someone go ahead of you today.

Brainstorm: *Let someone with only a few items cut in front of you in line at the store, or let someone get into an elevator or onto the bus first.*

For Reflection

Have you ever felt so rushed that you couldn't even fathom letting someone else go in front of you?

How do you feel when you're rushing, and how does your mood affect the people around you?

Might the potential for a positive, happy interaction outweigh the potential to lose a few minutes?

How Did It Go?

How did the other person respond when you let them go first? Did it benefit you in any way to slow down enough to do this?

JANUARY 13

Challenge

Introduce yourself to a neighbor you've never met, or don't know well.

Brainstorm: *Say hi when you're both taking the trash out, or, if it's currently warm where you live, sit on your front porch for a while after work so you'll see them when they come home. (Bonus: Relaxing outside is also an act of kindness to yourself!)*

For Reflection

Are there any neighbors you regularly see but have never formally met?

What's stopped you from introducing yourself before?

What's something you've noticed about this person's demeanor, appearance, or home that you could compliment?

How Did It Go?

Did you learn anything about your neighbor that interested or surprised you?

JANUARY 14

Challenge

Keep an eye out for someone who looks stressed or sad—a friend, a coworker, or even a stranger—and say something that might make this person laugh or smile.

For Reflection

When was the last time another person lifted your spirits when you were feeling down or overwhelmed?

What did they say or do, and why did it make you smile?

Did you learn anything from that experience that can help you lift someone else's spirits today?

How Did It Go?

Who did you uplift today? What can you learn from this experience to help others—or even yourself—smile more and stress less?

I recently traveled to Malaysia for a friend's wedding. The people were kind and warm, the culture rich, the trip magical. On my last day in Kuala Lumpur, I was headed out to buy souvenirs for family and friends when I stumbled across the most beautiful temple. I wandered around, overcome with majesty, trying to breathe it all in. I was still under the temple's spell when someone spoke to me.

"Your dress is ugly."

I looked to my right where the voice had come from. A woman was sitting on a bench, not looking in my direction. "Sorry?" I said, thinking I must have misheard.

She waved me off. I stood there for a moment, trying to decide on a course of action. She was American, the first and only other American I'd met during my trip.

Had she really just said my dress was ugly? *Maybe she said my dress was pretty,* I thought. I must have misunderstood.

"Did you just say my dress is ugly?" I asked.

"Yeah," she said. "I did."

I took a deep breath and replied, calmly, "Why would you say that to me?"

"I'm entitled to my opinion," she said. "Your dress is ugly; I can tell it's not well made. Your purse is dirty. I am free to voice my thoughts, and those are my thoughts about you."

To say it felt like getting slapped in the face would be an understatement; it was more of a punch to the gut. My blood boiled, my heart raced, but still I kept my voice at an even keel.

"You are entitled to your own opinion," I said. "But we also live in congress with other human beings. Why would you say something so aggressive and unkind?"

She reiterated her insults. Her words sliced coolly into the way I looked and the clothes I wore. That's when I said the one thing I regret saying.

"I wish there were fewer Americans like you traveling abroad," I told her. "You give the rest of us a bad name."

I turned and walked away, and she yelled one more barb at my back as I walked out of the temple. My hands were shaking as I walked down the street. I felt a strange knot of emotions in my chest: hurt, anger, fear. Why did this woman choose to attack me? Why had she said what she said?

I had just read the wonderful convocation address given by George Saunders to the Syracuse class of 2013. Saunders talks about something he calls a "failure of kindness," and those three words were very much on my mind. Yes, you could say I had suffered from a failure of kindness. But what I realized was that I, too, had been unkind.

I wish I hadn't said what I said to her. That came from a place of being wounded, of feeling the need to fight back. I wish I had said: "I hope the people you meet are kind."

Because I do hope that for her. I hope that she is bathed in loving-kindness, that she is inundated with so much that she cannot help but share it with the world.

While it's true that kindness engenders kindness, the lack of it can be a powerful teacher. For my remaining hours in Kuala Lumpur, I was abundantly kind to everyone I met. I complimented a girl on her joyful spirit, told shop owners how beautiful their merchandise was, smiled widely and genuinely. I made a point to be kind to these warm, generous people who had so kindly shared their country with me.

And every time I was shown kindness, no matter how small, I felt immeasurably grateful. That woman gave me a great gift. She reminded me that we all have a choice to be kind, and we are presented with that choice many times a day.

JANUARY 15

Challenge

Respond kindly to someone who is unkind to you.

For Reflection

What's your knee-jerk reaction when someone is unkind to you?

Does it soften your anger to consider that there may be a cause that doesn't condone but at least explains the person's behavior?

How would you respond instead if you were "being the change you wish to see" in the world?

How Did It Go?

How did the unkind person react when you treated them with more consideration than they offered you? How did you feel as a result?

JANUARY 16

Challenge

Say yes to a request when you're tempted to say no.

Note: *Be aware of your own needs, and make sure saying yes doesn't compromise your ability to meet them.*

For Reflection

What types of requests do you frequently decline?

Why do you say no to these types of requests?

Could you give a little without overextending yourself, so that instead of saying no, you say, "I can't do that, but I *can* do this."

How Did It Go?

Which request did you agree to meet, and what did you (and the other person) gain as a result?

JANUARY 17

Challenge

Call or Skype one of your grandparents or another older relative who may enjoy connecting with you and appreciate that you thought of them.

For Reflection

When was the last time you contacted this person? Were they pleased to hear from you?

Do you regularly connect with this person? If not, why?

How might it benefit you, and the other person, to prioritize staying in touch?

How Did It Go?

Was this person excited to hear from you? What did you discuss?

JANUARY 18

Challenge

Think about the kindest thing someone ever did for you. Below, write what happened and how this affected your life, and also identify anyone else who indirectly benefited from this act. List as many people as you can, and how specifically they benefited. Keep this in mind as you go about your day to remind yourself that one act of kindness can help more people than you know.

Brainstorm: *For example, if someone supported you when you were struggling with alcoholism and helped you get into treatment, this likely also benefited your family, your clients at work, and everyone whose lives you touched because you got sober.*

How Did It Go?

Before this exercise, did you realize how many people benefited from this act of kindness? Did recalling this experience inspire any specific acts of kindness today?

JANUARY 19

Challenge

Do something to make your life easier today.

Brainstorm: *Ask someone for help with something, cancel something you don't absolutely have to do, or decide to let something go instead of dwelling on it.*

For Reflection

What part of your day are you most dreading, and why?

Are you putting any unnecessary pressures on yourself, and why?

How would it affect your day and your state of mind if you took the pressure off?

How Did It Go?

What did you do to make your day easier? How did you benefit from this act of kindness?

JANUARY 20

Challenge

Smile and say good morning to everyone you encounter when you arrive at work, or wherever you're going today, to start everyone's day with positive energy.

For Reflection

What little things help you start your day with a smile?

Can you incorporate these things into your morning routine to create positive energy that you can then share?

Is there anything you currently do in the morning that starts your day with stress, and can you eliminate this or do it differently?

How Did It Go?

Did other people seem to appreciate your positive energy? How did it affect your day to start it with this positivity?

JANUARY 21

Challenge

Comment on a friend's or relative's picture on Facebook: "You look absolutely beautiful," or e-mail a photo of the two of you together, along with this compliment.

For Reflection

Has anyone ever done this for you? If so, how did you feel as a result?

Is there anything that you believe makes someone look beautiful aside from physical beauty?

When was the last time you told someone they looked beautiful? How do you think this made them feel?

How Did It Go?

What was your friend's reaction? Whether they reacted or not, how did you feel after paying the compliment?

The year I made my way to Galveston was the year I learned to see. I had a great job at an oil company in south Texas. "We" were the ones working hard and earning what we deserved. "They" were the lazy do-nothings who caused our kids to ask uncomfortable questions.

That year, they were everywhere in Galveston—panhandling on street corners, hustling at gas stations. And now that it was December, they were out in full force ringing little bells by their little red money pots. They never even bothered to say thanks when I threw in some change. Fine. We all know what "they" do with spare change anyway.

When I got home, I saw a big red bow at my door. A delivery for me! And how generous of my employer to send a fruit basket the size of a theme park. What on earth was I going to do with all that fruit? My freezer wasn't big enough to hold that much banana bread. So I did what I always do with things I don't want—I decided to give it away.

I took the driver's seat. The fruit basket took up the whole backseat. I was driving down Broadway, and it suddenly occurred to me that I had no idea where all this fruit and I were going. I had just moved here, and I wasn't exactly on popping-in-at-Christmas terms with anybody yet. Why not give it to a homeless person? They're all over the place. I could totally make somebody's day and warm my heart with my own good deed.

Rounding a corner just a few blocks east of the seawall, I saw two men and a woman sitting on the sidewalk. They were cracking open small pumpkins on the edge of the concrete, digging out the insides with their bare hands, and eating the pumpkins like watermelon. All I could think about was the Christmas turkey defrosting in my fridge. I thought about the forty-four cents I had just tossed at the jingle bell Santa. I thought about how huffy I got when I didn't get a thank-you.

I stopped the car. It was getting dark, and I had to watch my step with this giant fruit basket in my face. Peeking my head around, I blurted, "Can I wish you a Merry Christmas?"

"Look at that thing! Bring it on over!" They helped me set the basket down in all the pumpkin guts. Then one of the guys reached into his pocket and said, "Can we wish you a Merry Christmas too?" He pulled out a bright, gaudy silver bracelet from the interior of his jacket and offered it to me saying, "Thank you for this."

I rolled the bracelet slowly up my wrist. Then I shook his hand and said, "No—thank *you*."

Maybe it was Christmas. Maybe it was sitting around pumpkin guts trading fruit and trinkets with absolute strangers. Or maybe it was just that I went with it. But "they" suddenly became "we" that night. In the end, what really separates us? All I know is that for that one night, the entire playing field evened out. As soon as I took off my black-and-white goggles, I knew I was home in that warm, gaudy, silvery gray world.

Extending that circle of "we" can happen any time, anywhere. It happens for me every Christmas. People see me as the woman from Galveston decked out in the same gaudy silver bracelet every year. But actually, I'm the one marking the night that I first learned to see.

JANUARY 22

Challenge

Identify someone you think of as part of "they"—a group of people you see as separate from you—and start a friendly conversation with that person to bridge the gap.

For Reflection

Which group of people do you see as most separate from you, and why?

What type of judgments have you formed about them?

Even if just for today, can you consider that maybe none of those judgments are true?

How Did It Go?

What, if anything, made this challenge difficult for you, and what made it rewarding?

JANUARY 23

Challenge

Say something kind to someone you dislike, or do something kind for them.

Brainstorm: *Compliment a surly coworker on one of their strengths, or offer to help a neighbor who often seems confrontational.*

For Reflection

How do you usually treat people you dislike?

Are you proud of anything you often do when approaching people you dislike? Where do you have room for improvement?

What's one reminder about people or life that will help you be kind toward someone you dislike today?

How Did It Go?

How did the other person respond to your act of kindness? Did this change how you see or feel about them?

JANUARY 24

Challenge

Ask someone who serves you in some way, "How's your day going?"

For Reflection

Do you usually ask people this question when they serve you?

If so, do you wait for an answer, or say it more as a formality?

When someone asks you this while you're working, do you assume they don't really care to hear the answer—and what would they need to do differently to show they really do?

How Did It Go?

Did asking this question make you think about the server differently? Did the server seem to appreciate that you asked?

JANUARY 25

Challenge

Send an uplifting card to a sick child through a site like www.sendkidstheworld.com, www.cardsforhospitalizedkids.com, or www.hugsandhope.org.

For Reflection

What do you imagine a child who's hospitalized with a disease might feel on a daily basis?

How might your card make a difference in their day?

What could you write (or draw!) to bring a smile to a child's face?

How Did It Go?

Did you buy a card, or make one? Did it brighten your day to know you brightened a child's day?

JANUARY 26

Challenge

Write down one negative belief you hold about yourself, and then flip it into a positive affirmation that's kinder. Repeat this affirmation mentally throughout the day.

Brainstorm: *For example, you could flip "I ruin all relationships" into "I learn from all my relationships so I can grow and be better for myself and others."*

For Reflection

What's one negative belief you hold, and why do you believe this about yourself?

How has holding on to this belief affected you in negative way?

How can you spin this into a positive affirmation—one that doesn't feel like lying to yourself?

How Did It Go?

How did it affect your state of mind and behavior to mentally repeat a positive affirmation throughout the day?

JANUARY 27

Challenge

Contact an old colleague to see what they've been up to and ask how they're enjoying their current job.

For Reflection

What did you enjoy and appreciate about working with this person in the past?

What have you missed most about working with them?

Why might they appreciate hearing from you now? How might it make their day better?

How Did It Go?

What did you and your old colleague discuss? Did you enjoy reconnecting with them?

JANUARY 28

Challenge

Schedule something into your day that will make you laugh or smile.

Brainstorm: *Watch your favorite sitcom, look through photos of a loved one's baby, or blast your favorite music and dance around. (You can find more ideas here: http://tinybuddha.com/smile)*

For Reflection

When was the last time you allowed yourself some time for something silly and fun?

How does it affect your day and your interactions with others when you prioritize moments of levity?

What's something that always uplifts your spirit?

How Did It Go?

Were you able to relax and enjoy this activity? If not, why? If so, how did it affect the rest of your day?

JANUARY 29

Challenge

Think of something important that a loved one did recently—a job interview, a first date, or a milestone event, for example—and get in touch with them to ask how it went.

For Reflection

When was the last time someone remembered something important in your life and reached out to ask about it?

How did you feel—in general and about the relationship—when they did this?

What, if anything, sometimes prevents you from remembering and inquiring about these kinds of things?

How Did It Go?

Was the other person touched that you remembered and cared enough to inquire about their important event?

JANUARY 30

Challenge

Make a small sacrifice for someone else.

Brainstorm: *Let your spouse have your leftover Chinese food, spend part of your lunch break helping a friend, or give the money you were going to spend on a coffee to a Salvation Army bell ringer.*

For Reflection

Can you think of a recent time when someone made a small sacrifice for you? What did you most appreciate about this?

Does it feel natural to sacrifice for someone else? If not, what do you think makes this difficult for you?

What do you think makes the difference between healthy sacrifice and unhealthy sacrifice?

How Did It Go?

What sacrifice did you make? How did you feel after doing this, and how did the other person respond?

JANUARY 31

Challenge

Clean or beautify a common space in your home, apartment building, or at work, as an act of kindness for everyone who shares that space.

For Reflection

Have you ever looked at a common space and wished someone else would clean or improve it?

Why would you have appreciated it if someone made the effort to do this?

Did it occur to you to do this yourself? If not, why? What can you do to improve the space?

How Did It Go?

How do you think the space looks now? Did anyone notice or appreciate your efforts?

MONTHLY REVIEW

- Which challenges were the most helpful for you, and why?
- Which challenges were the most difficult for you, and why?
- What did you learn about yourself through the process of completing these challenges? Did you form any new insights about kindness, and living from an attitude of thoughtfulness?
- What did you learn about the people in your life?
- Did these challenges strengthen your relationships, and how?
- Did you identify any areas for improvement and growth?
- Head over to http://tinybuddha.com/love-forums to share your experiences with other readers!

FEBRUARY

Compassion and Understanding

Reflections from MELISSA LOPEZ

My friend had betrayed the trust of our shared group of friends by lying to save her reputation. She was so worried that everyone would judge her that she lied and contrived an entire story to support it. Ironically, the group judged her for lying instead of the indiscretion she tried to hide in the first place. Since she had maintained the deception for such a long time, everyone in the group couldn't see past this and alienated her for the dishonesty. In that moment, my friend lost all her friends.

After witnessing her loss, I couldn't abandon her. She was part of my life and I felt her pain far more deeply than any resentment I had against her. She needed me to stay by her side. So, despite what the group thought of her, I pushed it all aside and remained her friend. She spent many days depressed, crying, while I sat silently by her side.

Sometimes when the larger group wanted to hang out, it conflicted with my time with her. I started to feel pulled in different directions, especially when asked why I even wanted to be her friend anymore. My answer to that was "She is all alone and I'm her only friend," or I answered with this question, "How would you feel if you lost all your friends in an instant?" I always tried to bring about a gentle perspective to the situation so I wasn't perceived as taking sides. After time, the larger group of friends respected my choice to remain friends with her.

I always think about what could have happened had I not stayed by my friend's side. As social creatures, we have the basic need to belong and feel loved. Everyone has done something they regret, and nobody wants to feel alone in their pain. When you love someone, you comfort them in their pain regardless of any differences you may have. Even if you say nothing and you are just there by their side, you are helping them pull through their sorrow tremendously.

Reflections from AMY CONNORS

You never know what a person is carrying. No one would suspect that in my brand-new, shiny leather bag there were five letters from my brother, who is in prison. I am the oldest of five and we lost our parents, so he is like a son to me. The pain contained in those words, those letters, in that bag, was heavy. His story is the heartbreak of my life. When I think about Michael, I fight the tears back every time.

People seem shocked when I tell them about my past or that I have a sibling in prison or that my mother was murdered. These are things I don't discuss at dinner parties or in hallways. At thirty-eight, I now have all the trappings of a wonderful life, but the road to getting "here" was fraught with an extraordinary amount of suffering. There was a major quest for the "why." Why me? What did I do to "deserve" all of this? Many tears and years later, I see that the suffering has been my greatest gift. It has allowed me to feel true and genuine compassion for all humans, even those I don't know. This understanding of the human condition leads my life today. Suffering is something every single person can relate to. It's our commonality.

We never know what people have in their "bag." Regardless of how they look, we don't know the road they've been down. When you encounter someone at a store and they seem rude, could you stop for a moment and have compassion? Could you just stop and think, *Hey, I don't know what this guy went through this morning. He could have just gotten diagnosed with cancer*? You just never know. That's not to say that it's okay for people to take their anger out on others. It's simply to say that when we look at others with a compassionate heart, we see a shift within ourselves, we expand our ability to love, and lessen our own suffering.

FEBRUARY 1

Challenge

Before all conversations today, think of one way that you're similar to the person you're speaking with to help you approach them with empathy.

For Reflection

What are some things you have in common with every other human being?

How does it change your feelings about people who seem different to consider our commonality?

How might it improve your interactions if you approached people with this in mind?

How Did It Go?

Did going into conversations with an empathetic mind-set change how you approached them?

FEBRUARY 2

Challenge

Ask someone you encounter today, "How are you feeling?" If they respond with "fine," ask follow-up questions to let them know you truly care to hear if they're feeling something else.

For Reflection

How often do you answer this question with "fine" because you feel unable or scared to share your real feelings?

How would it comfort you to know someone really cares and wants to understand?

How might you be able to make others feel more comfortable opening up and sharing their feelings? Is there a better question to ask than "How are you doing?"

How Did It Go?

Did the other person give you a detailed response? Did this connection feel more meaningful than other conversations you've had with this person in the past?

FEBRUARY 3

Challenge

Instead of treating someone how you want to be treated, ask them how *they* want to be treated, and do that.

Brainstorm: *For example, if someone seems upset and you'd want to be left alone if you were feeling that way, say, "When I'm upset, I like to be left alone. Is that what you want as well?" Or, if someone seems confused and you'd want advice if you were in their shoes, say, "I like to get lots of perspectives when I'm confused. Do you want my opinion, or do you just want a sounding board?"*

For Reflection

Have you ever assumed someone wanted to be treated as you'd want to be treated, and then realized you were wrong?

How might it improve your relationships if you better understood what others want from you and, therefore, were better able to meet their needs and expectations?

How Did It Go?

Did you learn that someone else's wants differ from yours? How did you act on what you learned?

FEBRUARY 4

Challenge

Think about how it shows in your body language and facial expressions when you're feeling the emotions listed below, and write the physical manifestation next to each emotion. Keep this knowledge in mind as you go about your day so that you may better recognize when someone is feeling something painful. (Of course, everyone is different—but remember, we're a lot more alike than we often realize!)

Stress:

Shame:

Anger:

Fear:

Distrust:

How Did It Go?

Were you able to respond to anyone more gently than you may have by keeping an eye out for physical signs of emotional pain?

FEBRUARY 5

Challenge

Whenever you get hard on yourself today, comfort yourself with a physical gesture and a few words of compassion, such as, "I'm having a tough time, but I deserve my own love and kindness." According to self-compassion researcher Kristin Neff, physical touch releases the feel-good hormone oxytocin—even when the touch is your own.

Brainstorm: *Rub your arm, rest your cheek on your hand, or put both hands over your heart.*

For Reflection

What do you usually do when you start getting hard on yourself? How does this keep you stuck?

What, if anything, do you fear might happen if you're *not* hard on yourself? Is it possible that's not true?

What type of physical gesture do you find most soothing?

How Did It Go?

Did you comfort yourself with physical touch today? If so, did calming your body help calm your mind and enable you to be kinder to yourself?

FEBRUARY 6

Challenge

Share a relevant story with a loved one who is struggling in order to show them you can relate, and that they're not alone in what they're going through.

For Reflection

Has anyone ever shared a story from their life to let you know they could relate to what you were going through?

What did you feel when they admitted that they'd been there before?

How did you feel toward them after they opened up in this way?

How Did It Go?

What story did you share? Did this seem to comfort the other person? Did you feel closer to them after this interaction?

FEBRUARY 7

Challenge

Pay attention to what the people around you seem to be feeling, physically or emotionally, and give someone something tangible they might need.

Brainstorm: *Give someone working on or outside your home a glass of water, bring a healthy snack to a coworker who's working on a deadline and hasn't been able to take lunch, or lend your stress ball or a soothing scented candle to someone who seems stressed.*

For Reflection

Do you ever find it difficult to identify and meet your needs when you're caught up in your daily routine?

Has anyone ever supplied something you needed right when you needed it most? If so, how did that simple act make a difference in your day?

Why might your loved ones appreciate knowing that you're paying attention and looking out for their needs?

How Did It Go?

What need did you meet, and for whom? How do you think this affected that person's state of mind and improved their day?

I was walking my dog in my neighborhood when a group of kids that I knew as troublemakers approached me in the street outside my house. One of them, a young boy about ten years old, threatened me with an empty liquor bottle raised in his hand. He used the most horrifying profanity and accused me of keeping the ball that they'd apparently kicked into my backyard.

He was so aggressive that at first I felt afraid, but in deciding how to respond in this situation, I realized I had two choices: I could either respond with fear or with love. To respond with fear, I could have threatened him back, told him to get lost, and that I would call the police. However, as I played that scenario out in my mind, I realized that a fearful response would only escalate the situation.

While not the easiest or most instinctive choice, I decided to respond with love and let myself feel compassion for this boy. I wondered why such a young guy was so full of anger and hate. I felt sad to think that maybe he didn't have a secure and happy life at home.

Having compassion helped me to speak gently. I told him that there was no reason to get upset and that I'd be happy to look in my garden for his ball. He seemed surprised by my response and quickly calmed down. I was able to give him back his ball and the group of kids thanked me, apologized, and went on their way.

Now, whenever I'm in situations when people aren't very nice to me or I haven't been very nice to them, I ask myself, *What is the motivator? Love or fear?* It does wonders for developing empathy, compassion, and forgiveness. Having the courage to choose compassion and love over fear means that those kids now smile and wave at me when they see me. Imagine the kind of world we'd live in if we all chose love over fear.

My life was already carefully planned in my head. I had one semester left to finish my university degree, but mainly, I wanted to live my dream and continue working with competition horses. Then I had an accident: my horse slipped and fell, taking me down with him, resulting in a simple fracture that left me walking on crutches for three years. During that time, everything went wrong.

Those three difficult years taught me more about life than I had ever learned. However, they taught me even more about people and compassion. My family helped out and friends supported me, understandably, but there were other, unexpected people who taught me what true compassion is—people who had no good reason to cope with my emotional struggling but did.

My physiotherapists—strangers at the beginning—became not only friends but family. Instead of just doing their job and treating my ankle, they helped me when I was most vulnerable and gave me the strength to keep going. They listened, put me back on track when I lost hope, and were always there whenever I needed them, both physically and emotionally. Their help and support went well beyond their working hours and duty as therapists. Showing compassion for a friend you've known for years is easy. I learned what love really is by watching my therapists support a "stranger" in such a way that they became among the most important people in my life.

The Greeks have several words for love, among them *agape,* love for humanity. Unconditional, selfless love much like compassion. Love that gives, yet expects nothing in return. Love for the sake of love. We do not need to know a person to give love. Everyone is facing a battle we do not know about. But we don't need to know the details to love and help, to support and encourage. We only need to extend our hands and show that we care. True compassion does not start with the people we know. On the contrary, we need to open our hearts and show kindness to every single person we meet.

FEBRUARY 8

Challenge

Identify one person, group of people, or type of people you believe doesn't deserve your compassion. Now try to empathize with why those people may be like they are or may do the things they do. Think of all possible factors that may have contributed—their past struggles, their physical or emotional health, their disadvantages. Write these things below to help you challenge the belief that this person or these people don't deserve compassion.

How Did It Go?

Was this eye-opening for you? Do you feel better able to offer compassion? If not, how could you overcome your remaining blocks?

FEBRUARY 9

Challenge

When someone says or does something that hurts or offends you, instead of assuming the worst, consider that you misunderstood them and ask, "What was your intention?"

For Reflection

Have you ever felt that someone judged your actions and misunderstood your intention?

How would it have made a difference if that person gave you a chance to share this?

How might your relationships improve if you always sought clarification before jumping to conclusions—and if others followed your lead?

How Did It Go?

Did you learn that someone's intention differed from your assumption? If so, did this help you avoid unnecessary conflict and better understand each other?

FEBRUARY 10

Challenge

Use Martha Beck's "reverse engineering" method of developing empathy today. Identify someone you'd like to understand better. Now think of a specific interaction when you had trouble understanding what they were feeling. Imitate their body language and facial expressions, and to the best of your ability repeat their words using the same tone they used. This will allow you to better understand them, as odds are, you'll feel the same thing they felt.

For Reflection

Who in your life do you often struggle to understand, and why?

How has your inability to understand them impacted your relationship?

How might your relationship improve if you made a stronger effort to understand what they feel, and then acted on what you learned?

How Did It Go?

What did you feel when you "reverse engineered" the situation? Did you form any new insights about the other person through this exercise?

FEBRUARY 11

Challenge

Instead of beating yourself up for something you feel you could have done better, reward yourself for doing it at all.

For Reflection

Do you more frequently commend yourself for your efforts or berate yourself for them? If you chose the latter, why do you think you do this?

How does it negatively affect you to focus on the ways you believe you're falling short?

How might your life improve if you rewarded yourself for your efforts and felt good about them—and yourself—as a result?

How Did It Go?

How did it affect your mind-set and your day to shift from self-flagellation to self-appreciation?

FEBRUARY 12

Challenge

Ask someone a creative question to better understand them.

Brainstorm: *Some examples include: "What would do with your life if money was no object?" "If you could change one thing about yourself, what would it be?" "If you could go back in time, would you do anything differently?"*

For Reflection

What's the most thought-provoking question someone ever asked you about yourself?

Did you feel closer to this person after answering this? Did you feel they better understood you?

What do you think you convey to someone else when you ask questions to better understand their desires, fears, and regrets?

How Did It Go?

What question did you ask, and did the answer surprise you? Do you feel you understand this person a little better now?

FEBRUARY 13

Challenge

If you discover someone who is hurting in some way, use physical touch to show your empathy and care.

For Reflection

Do you regularly use physical touch to show others you care? If not, what has prevented you from being physical in this way in the past?

Can you remember a time when a loving touch helped you feel less hurt and alone?

Why do you think this sign of empathy and care comforted you?

How Did It Go?

Was the other person open to your affection? Did it seem to help them? How did you feel when offering it?

FEBRUARY 14

Challenge

Offer words of compassion to someone who frequently complains instead of avoiding them or judging them for being negative.

For Reflection

Have you ever felt like people were avoiding or judging you because you were unhappy with an aspect of your life and complaining a lot as a result?

If so, how would you have preferred other people respond to you?

What do you think makes the difference between enabling someone who tends to ruminate on the negative and showing them compassion?

How Did It Go?

Did your compassion seem to help the other person? Do you think your positive response may have softened their negativity somewhat?

I never had what one might call a strong sibling bond with my brother. When we were kids, my perception of him was that he intensely disliked me, and in turn I behaved in a similar manner toward him.

A few years ago we had the opportunity to see each other in a very different light. By this time I was becoming aware of psychology and of different personalities in general. My findings led me to conclude that high sensitivity and avoidant personality traits ran in the family, which in our case meant rarely discussing our feelings and emotions. I also gathered that my brother was susceptible to anxiety in certain circumstances, but I didn't realize just how deeply affected he was.

One day, we were invited to a small party at a relative's house. I noticed nothing unusual about my brother's behavior; we all seemed to have a great time. The day after the party my brother and I headed home separately. I was already halfway home when I received a phone call from him. I could barely make sense of what he was trying to say; he was so engulfed by panic. I could just make out his cry: "*Help me please.*"

I rushed to where he was and found him on the side of the road, where he was paralyzed by fear. I'd never seen him like that before, and my heart ached when I imagined what must have led him to that state. I took him to the hospital, and while we were in the waiting room, he confessed he'd been suffering panic attacks for a while and was finding it hard to cope with daily life.

After that, we went back to our parents' house. We had a very long chat, not only about this incident, but about things that happened in the past that caused friction between us. That's when things started to fall into place—our stories were not so different. The common thread—dysfunctionality of our family—had taken such a toll on our relationship that we couldn't be honest with each other. Hence my brother's perceived arrogance was only a façade behind which to hide. At the same time I had found it hard to get close to him and made no attempts to understand why this was so. Now we were mutually acknowledging where we went wrong and made an effort to put years' sorrows right.

Ever since that incident I respond differently when we have a disagreement. I picture him by the roadside to remind me of his vulnerability and that there's always a reason for his actions, even if I don't understand it. With this kind of compassion, we've moved on to a better relationship. Even though there's still a lot to be resolved, we made a start by understanding what makes each other tick.

FEBRUARY 15

Challenge

Write "hurt people hurt people" on a Band-Aid and stick it somewhere you'll see often, to remind yourself that the most difficult people are often in the most pain.

For Reflection

Can you think of a time when you hurt other people because you were in pain? How might it have helped you if other people understood this and cut you some slack?

Now think of a difficult person that you've encountered. Is it possible they were dealing with their own hurt?

How might it change your feelings and actions to consider this before approaching a "difficult" person?

How Did It Go?

Did you see people differently as a result of this exercise? If so, did it change how you responded to them?

FEBRUARY 16

Challenge

Make it a goal to say "I see where you're coming from" to someone at least once today—and really mean it.

For Reflection

Can you think of a recent time when it felt like someone didn't see your side?

How would you have felt had they said this to you?

How does it improve your interactions when both sides try to see where the other person is coming from?

How Did It Go?

Were you able to see where the other person was coming from? If not, what prevented you from seeing their side?

FEBRUARY 17

Challenge

Buy a compassionately made product.

Brainstorm: *For example, buy certified humane eggs, makeup not tested on animals, or fair trade goods.*

For Reflection

Do you ordinarily make it a priority to buy compassionately made products?

Do you believe this makes a difference in the world? Why or why not?

How Did It Go?

What product did you buy? Do you think you might do this regularly going forward?

FEBRUARY 18

Challenge

Complete the writing prompts below. Keep these things in mind as you go about your day to help you treat yourself with compassion.

I wouldn't treat others as harshly as I treat myself because. . .

My loved ones wouldn't treat me like I treat myself because. . .

To treat myself better, I'd need to let go of. . .

I can start letting go by. . .

How Did It Go?

Did you form any helpful new insights in completing this exercise? Did you do anything differently—and feel differently—today as a result?

FEBRUARY 19

Challenge

Convey to someone today that you understand their feelings.

Brainstorm: *For example, you could say, "I can imagine that was frustrating for you," or "I totally understand why you'd feel irritated; I'd feel that way too if I were in your shoes."*

For Reflection

How do you feel—about yourself, your circumstances, and the other person—when it seems that someone just doesn't get what you're feeling, and why?

How do you feel when someone expresses that they understand the way you feel, and they'd feel the same way if they were in your shoes?

What's something you could say or do to better understand what others are feeling so that you can validate and comfort them in this way?

How Did It Go?

Did the other person seem relieved when you validated their feelings?

FEBRUARY 20

Challenge

Think about someone you know who could use some help, and then ask a mutual friend if they'll work with you to support that person.

For Reflection

Have you ever felt like you were powerless to help someone because you didn't know what to do?

Did you consider asking a mutual friend to help you offer support?

If not, how may it have made a difference if you had?

How Did It Go?

Who did you decide to help? What ideas did you and your mutual friend come up with, and were any of them things you wouldn't have considered on your own?

FEBRUARY 21

Challenge

Devote five to twenty minutes to a simple compassion mediation. Start by visualizing someone toward whom you easily feel compassion, and silently repeat the words *May you be happy and free from pain and suffering*. Now visualize yourself and mentally repeat the same thing. Next, visualize someone toward whom you have neutral feelings while repeating these same well wishes. After that, visualize someone for whom you have trouble feeling compassion, to help extend the goodwill you've fostered toward them. End the meditation by extending your well wishes to everyone on the planet, with these words: *May all living beings be happy and free from suffering*.

Tip: *If you Google "Metta Meditation," you'll find countless scripts and tutorials online.*

How Did It Go?

Were you able to feel compassion during this meditation? How did this affect your interactions today?

A friend had spent the day observing my Pilates teacher as part of his medical training. I was excited for him to see the benefits of her work, so I was shocked when she said that my friend hijacked a couple of her lessons. Instead of observing the way Pilates would help with the students' problems, he halted their lessons and did body work on them.

I was aghast. I hate confrontation, but I had to ask him about it. How could he do this? His answer blew me away. He said, "I got scared, so I reacted in the same way I always do when I panic. I took over." This took me a while to absorb, because it is exactly the opposite of my fear response.

Understanding my friend's response completely shifted the way I look at people, especially when they are behaving "badly." I had learned that people fall into one of six personality patterns that automatically generate negative responses to stress. I understood it abstractly, but my friend's shocking statement illuminated this reaction mechanism.

What a revelation! Our ugliest behavior is just a knee-jerk reaction to a deep fear that there is something wrong with us. According to their personality patterns, some people become dictators, others become drama queens, some turn into whiny victims, others blame everyone else. And, no matter how ineffective or nonsensical their actions, this is their best attempt to overcome that awful fear.

I gained instant compassion for my friend. He was just scared! From that point forward, whenever his inner dictator reared its head, I was able to react with kindness and understanding instead of confusion and judgment. That shift was a huge gift for our friendship. But I also gained an invaluable tool that I still use all the time. When someone behaves negatively, I silently ask, *What are they scared of?* and *How is this behavior an attempt to overcome their fear that something is wrong with them?*

When my defeatist friend digs in her heels and insists that nothing will ever work for her, I can hear her survival mechanism screaming, *If you're stupid enough to believe you'll succeed this time, you'll only be disappointed again!* When another friend becomes aloof and dismissive, I see her panic and know that she only can feel safe again by putting up her sky-high walls. When my friend's mom offers me food I've already refused five times, I see her desperately trying to cover up the feeling that she isn't good enough. And, in all these cases, I'm much more able to respond with kindness and compassion.

FEBRUARY 22

Challenge

Whenever someone upsets you today, instead of snapping at them or acting hurt, ask yourself, *What fears may cause them to act as they do?*

For Reflection

Have you ever done things you're not proud of because you were scared?

Did you realize at the time that there was fear behind your actions?

How does it change your perception of others to realize they may be motivated by fear?

How Did It Go?

What fear did you identify as a potential motivator behind someone's actions? How did this affect how you responded to them?

FEBRUARY 23

Challenge

Let someone off the hook for a mistake or shortcoming that won't be a big deal in the grand scheme of things.

For Reflection

Have you ever wished people would choose their battles more wisely and cut you some slack?

How do you feel, in general and about yourself, when people nitpick and point out things you could have done better?

What would you rather people say and do when you know you messed up?

How Did It Go?

For what minor transgression did you let someone off the hook, and what happened as a result? What would have happened if you had chosen to nitpick instead?

FEBRUARY 24

Challenge

Identify someone in your life who hasn't always shown you compassion, and do something compassionate for them.

For Reflection

Do you feel resistance to offering this person compassion, and if so, why?

What's one reason they may need an act of compassion?

How might it improve your relationship if you offer them the compassion they haven't offered you?

How Did It Go?

What did you do to display compassion? Did the other person respond in a way that surprised you?

FEBRUARY 25

Challenge

Write below one or two things you've done recently that you feel bad about. Then list for each one a potential need you may have been trying to meet in order to better understand the valid intentions instead of condemning the misguided actions.

Brainstorm: *If you overate, you may have been trying to distract yourself from painful feelings; if you got defensive and argued with a friend, you may have been trying to protect yourself from pain you experienced in a past friendship.*

Action:

Need:

Action:

Need:

How Did It Go?

How did you feel about yourself and your actions after recognizing and empathizing with the needs you were trying to meet?

FEBRUARY 26

Challenge

Text someone who you know has been struggling lately, "I've been thinking of you, and I'm here if you need me!"

For Reflection

Have you ever wished that someone would say this to you?

Have you considered saying this to someone but stopped yourself? If so, why?

What do you think you convey to a friend about your relationship and your feelings for them with a simple reminder text like this?

How Did It Go?

Who did you text, and how did they respond? Do you think you made a positive difference in their day?

FEBRUARY 27

Challenge

Think of a problem you've been obsessing about. Now identify someone else who's also affected by this problem. Ask them what it's been like for them so you can better understand and potentially help instead of focusing on yourself and your own feelings.

Brainstorm: *If you've been stressed about moving, you could ask your spouse to share his or her thoughts and fears about this; if you've been anxious about an impending change in management at work, you could ask some coworkers how they've been feeling about this.*

For Reflection

Can you think of a recent time when you obsessed about a challenge that also affected the people around you? Did you stop to consider how this impacted them? If not, why?

How might it have benefited you to focus on someone other than yourself?

Assuming the people around you were feeling the same things as you, why might they have appreciated your attention and concern?

How Did It Go?

Do you think you helped the other person (or people)? Was this also helpful to you? If so, how and why?

FEBRUARY 28

Challenge

Leave a compassionate response on a blog post or social media update in which someone expresses sadness, frustration, or any other type of overwhelming emotion.

For Reflection

Do you usually empathize when people publicly share their emotions, or do you tend to form judgments, and why?

What do you imagine someone might be feeling or seeking when they share their emotions publicly?

Have you ever been helped or encouraged by a thoughtful comment on your blog or social media page? What did you most appreciate about this?

How Did It Go?

What did you write, and did this differ from your initial reaction?

FEBRUARY 29

Challenge

Tell someone who's rushing for your benefit "Take your time—there's no rush!" to help alleviate their anxiety about potentially inconveniencing you.

Brainstorm: *You could say this to someone who's running late, to someone who's telling you a story and struggling to express themselves, or to a customer service representative who's having difficulty with their computer.*

For Reflection

Do you regularly do this, or are you more apt to rush people? If you chose the latter, why do you think you do this?

How do you feel when you suspect someone else is getting impatient with you?

What would you most appreciate about hearing "take your time" when you're feeling pressured to rush?

How Did It Go?

Who did you say this to, and did they seem relieved?

MONTHLY REVIEW

- Which challenges were the most helpful for you, and why?
- Which challenges were the most difficult for you, and why?
- What did you learn about yourself through the process of completing these challenges? Did you form any new insights about compassion, and living from an attitude of understanding?
- What did you learn about the people in your life?
- Did these challenges strengthen your relationships, and how?
- Did you identify any areas for improvement and growth?
- Head over to http://tinybuddha.com/love-forums to share your experiences with other readers!

MARCH

Authenticity and Vulnerability

Reflections from KARINA KAINTH

Habitually, I have been a person of words more than gestures. I value deep conversations in my relationships. This has traditionally served as my language of love. I always thought that there was nothing wrong with seeking conversation rather than a heartfelt hug. But deep down, I knew that this self-ascribed declaration that I was not a "touchy-feely" person was holding me back.

I would shy away from hugs or kisses from my loving parents. I would write beautifully heartfelt cards for my best friend on her birthday but would feel uncomfortable when she would hug me to express her appreciation. There was a time and a place for physical displays of affection, I believed, and those times were few and far between.

I reached a breaking point at a personal development seminar where hugs were encouraged as a central element of the experience and were given out even more freely than conversation. People would enter the conference room and just run across to give others a smiling embrace. No words, just touch.

I soon grew frustrated in my isolation. I needed to get to know people, using my words, before just going and hugging them. Did no one else feel the way I did? The frustration turned to denial, and then peer pressure manifested in shame. *There must be something wrong with me,* I concluded. Why couldn't I just open up physically?

In a conversation with my mother one night during the conference, I explained my anxiety. She said something that seemed to still my heart: *There is strength in giving.*

I suddenly knew what had been holding me back. Physical affection, when offered earnestly, is a deep, raw form of expression. It is simply an exchange of energy—there is nothing to hide behind. I was afraid that by giving my love to others in this pure, unadulterated form, I'd be exposed. People would see my vulnerability, and they'd realize how desperately I needed love. But what I hadn't realized is that by allowing myself to give love and show my vulnerability, I was actually demonstrating my inner strength. In my embrace, my message didn't have to be: "I need love—please give it to me." Instead, it could be: "Here I stand, just as I am, full of love, seeking to join my love with yours."

Once I started to do this, hesitantly at first and then more confidently, I began to heal. Tapping someone on the shoulder and greeting him with an embrace made me feel empowered, not suppliant. Each one of the hugs I gave and received connected me to others at a soul level, in a way that mere words could not.

Opening yourself up and asking for love can feel incredibly scary. But when you come from a place of inner strength and self-love, knowing that you deserve what you are asking for, a hug can be a transformative exchange of two souls—at their most vulnerable and yet so very strong.

MARCH 1

Challenge

Greet someone with a hug today.

For Reflection

Do you usually feel comfortable hugging people?

If not, what thoughts, beliefs, fears, or insecurities contribute to your discomfort with hugs?

What do you think you convey to another person when you greet them with a smile and a hug?

How Did It Go?

How did it feel to greet someone physically with a hug instead of just your words? How did the person respond?

MARCH 2

Challenge

Maintain eye contact during a conversation
when you're tempted to look away.

For Reflection

What do you find uncomfortable about eye contact? For which reasons have you avoided prolonged eye contact in the past?

What have you feared others might see?

What would happen if they saw it, and loved you anyway?

How Did It Go?

How did maintaining eye contact affect the conversation and your state of mind?

MARCH 3

Challenge

Tell someone you care about how you feel about them, and why.

For Reflection

Who in your life might not realize how you feel about them or how much you care?

What exactly do you feel, and why do you value this relationship?

Why have you not shared this before, and what's the best thing that could happen if you share it now?

How Did It Go?

How did you feel when sharing your feelings, and how did the other person respond?

MARCH 4

Challenge

Think of a time when someone you love was vulnerable with you—a time when they shared a secret, a struggle, or their honest feelings. Write below why you appreciated this, how it benefited you to learn this about them and be there for them, and how it strengthened your relationship. Keep these things in mind today when you question whether it's worth letting your guard down and letting others in.

How Did It Go?

Did you form any new insights about the power of vulnerability? Did this affect how you engaged with others today?

MARCH 5

Challenge

Sit with a loved one in comfortable silence, with the goal of simply being there together.

For Reflection

What do you usually think or feel when sitting with someone in silence?

What do you usually do when things get quiet?

In which relationships do you find silence comfortable, and what could you learn from these relationships to make silence comfortable in others?

How Did It Go?

Did the silence feel comfortable, and if not, why do you think that was? What could have made it more comfortable?

MARCH 6

Challenge

Choose one thing you enjoy doing that you don't often share with others. Now invite someone else to experience it with you.

For Reflection

What has prevented you from inviting others to share this with you in the past?

How might the experience of doing this differ if you got to appreciate it with someone else who enjoyed it just as much?

What might someone else appreciate about doing this activity with you specifically?

How Did It Go?

What did you do today, and with whom? How did it enhance the experience to do it with another person?

MARCH 7

Challenge

Start a conversation with a stranger.

Brainstorm: *Comment on something about your shared experience (such as waiting in line or riding the bus), offer a compliment, or ask a question about something you notice about them (such as a unique hairstyle or new phone).*

For Reflection

How often do you start conversations with strangers?

How do you usually respond when a stranger starts a conversation with you?

Have you ever formed a friendship with someone who wasn't, at one point, a stranger?

How Did It Go?

What did you gain or learn through the experience of connecting with someone new?

I had just begun going to therapy, and one of my homework assignments was to step out of my comfort zone by making plans to go out with a friend. Coincidentally, or maybe not so much, a woman I hadn't seen since high school, seven years back, had recently moved back into town and gotten in touch with me. We made plans to meet for coffee one morning the following week.

We had a lot to catch up on—families, friends, partners, jobs. The conversation turned to health, and it was relevant to bring up my recent depression diagnosis. I had yet to tell almost anyone about it, even my closest friends, for fear of embarrassment and judgment. I struggled to decide whether or not it was necessary, appropriate, or unseemly. Being open and honest is frightening stuff.

I summoned all my courage and chose to take the risk, embrace my new objective to be authentic, and tell her about it. I expressed how I had been feeling low, started seeing a therapist, been diagnosed with depression, quit my job, and how this was all affecting my life. Much to my relief, I was not met with disappointment, aversion, or distaste. She responded by explaining her own struggles and challenges. It was a beautiful moment of shared vulnerability.

Without my initial risk of authenticity, we never would have connected in the meaningful way that we did. Now I call this the gift of going first, and it opens new opportunities for sharing and bonding. Of course it also opens new opportunities for judgment, discouragement, and hurt feelings; this risk is vulnerability. We must agree to be aggrieved sometimes so that we can be elated many a time. People look for vulnerability in others but are terrified to show it in themselves. By giving the gift of going first, the space is created for deep connection with others resulting in more understanding, compassion, and love.

My ex-husband left me three years ago after having an affair. It cut deeply, but I healed and moved on. I'm now in love with a man who also suffered deeply at the end of his marriage. The bond we found at the beginning was never one of bitterness or mutual wallowing, and that was a big attraction for us both. It could have been so easy for our common ground to be past pain, but we had so much more. What we have now is an amazing relationship filled with love and trust; but that only comes from allowing ourselves to be vulnerable, despite what has happened in our past.

We could never have found each other or shared such depth of love if we'd had protective walls built up. Because I am so happy now, my joy makes me very aware of all that I could have been missing had I let any of the big, bad fears stop me from finding love again. I've also had to restore trust in my ex-husband because he is the father of my children. When someone has betrayed you, it can be easy to see their every act, decision, or motive as suspicious in some way. But to do so is to build up that wall again. I've had to trust that he wants the same as me when it comes to our children, and dare to be vulnerable and speak up when things are not right for them. As a result, the children have handled the divorce and the changes to their lives relatively smoothly.

In order to get to a place where you are comfortable being vulnerable and trusting a person or situation, you must first be honest with yourself. It is not weak to admit to ourselves that we fear rejection. Once we look the big, bad fears in the eye and see they are simply trying to protect us from being hurt, we can simply say, "Thanks, but no thanks. I'd like to see what's beyond that wall."

MARCH 8

Challenge

Share a fear you've never shared before with someone who you think could help you overcome it.

For Reflection

Why have you kept this fear to yourself, and how has this limited you?

How would it feel to no longer be alone with this fear?

Who might you be and what might you do differently if this fear no longer limited you?

How do you think someone else would feel knowing they helped you make these changes?

How Did It Go?

How did you feel after sharing this? Does the fear feel less overwhelming now, and do you feel closer to the other person?

MARCH 9

Challenge

Display something in your workspace that represents a part of your authentic self that you may be tempted to keep separate from your "work self" (something not related to religion or politics). This will give your coworkers a chance to get to know you beyond your work persona.

Brainstorm: *Place a picture from your yoga retreat on your desk, or a mug emblazoned with a quote or character from your favorite book or movie.*

For Reflection

How do you believe you need to present yourself at work, and why?

Is there anything you hide or downplay to appear professional?

Would your work, and your relationships with coworkers, feel more fulfilling if you were able to reveal more pieces of your authentic self?

How Did It Go?

Did anyone comment on this particular item? If so, did this facilitate a conversation that felt more authentic or meaningful than usual?

MARCH 10

Challenge

Complete the writing prompt below. Then share this with someone, in real life or online at http://tinybuddha.com/love-forums, to help you work through your shame and break through the fear of how others will perceive this.

People would definitely judge me if they knew that I...

How Did It Go?

How did the other person respond? Did sharing this help you feel less shame about it?

MARCH 11

Challenge

Update one of your social media pages with your honest feelings about something going on in your life. (If you don't have any social media pages, e-mail someone to share your feelings.)

For Reflection

How often do you share what you're honestly feeling on your social media pages?

What prevents you from being authentic on social media?

How do you think the experience of using social media would differ if people were more honest?

How Did It Go?

What did you share? Did people respond, and if so, were any responses helpful to you?

MARCH 12

Challenge

Identify one experience from your childhood that taught you to hide your true self—some event that led you to believe that hiding was safest. As you go about your day, recognize when you're acting on this belief, and remind yourself, *I am not that child anymore, and this belief no longer serves me, since it holds me back in life.*

For Reflection

In what way did it serve you to hide yourself when you were a child?

How does hiding hinder or limit you now?

What do you stand to gain if you choose to more regularly share your true self?

How Did It Go?

Was this reminder helpful to you? Did you do anything you might not have done if not for this exercise?

MARCH 13

Challenge

Share something that is going on in your life with someone you don't usually open up to.

Brainstorm: *This could be something light, like an upcoming family visit you're looking forward to, or something heavier, like a legal battle or your impending divorce.*

For Reflection

Who in your life have you wanted to open up to, and what's held you back?

Has this person shared with you in this way before? If not, is it possible they're waiting for a sign you'd be comfortable with that?

What do you feel most comfortable sharing with them, and why?

How Did It Go?

What did you share, and how did the other person respond? How do you feel about this relationship after revealing more than you usually do?

MARCH 14

Challenge

Own up to a mistake, flaw, or shortcoming today, allowing others to see that you, too, are human, flawed, and imperfect.

For Reflection

Do you usually share your mistakes or try to hide them, and why?

What do you fear others may think about you if they learn about your mistakes, flaws, and shortcomings?

Has it ever been helpful to you to learn about someone else's mistake, flaw, or shortcoming, and why?

How Did It Go?

What mistake, flaw, or shortcoming did you share? Did this feel more empowering than you imagined it would?

Reflections from PAUL SANDERS

Several years ago, I was so unhappy with my loneliness that I decided I was going to try anything to build a social life and have friends who cared about me. I read all the books I could find and tried all the techniques they shared, but I still had to make a lot of effort to build friendships and hold my social life together. Then I started to learn and apply the principles of authenticity.

I used to think that I needed to be as extroverted as possible. It was exhausting, and people could see that it wasn't really how I wanted to present myself. As a celebration of my uniqueness, I started behaving calmer and more interested in the depth of things. While I became less gregarious, I actually started making more friends, and more genuine ones, and the relationships with them were solid.

I was amazed by those results; I knew that authenticity would contribute to my happiness, but never thought that being less of an upbeat, talkative person would improve my social life. When I met new people, I talked about what I wanted to talk about instead of saying what I thought other people wanted to hear.

Authenticity completely shifted the way I interacted with people and made my social life much easier to develop and maintain, and it all started with liking my authentic self. When you like your authentic self, you appreciate your uniqueness, and you recognize your imperfections, quirks, and mistakes. You know you can improve but will never be perfect, and you're okay with that. This means you won't take yourself too seriously and you'll show a side of you that is vulnerable and completely human. We all want to engage with people who can interact and relate without masks or barriers to hide behind—and that comes from liking yourself.

I recently ended a one-year relationship. About three months later I began to try to date again. Those months spent alone were crucial in helping me find myself. I began to feel whole and recentered, aware of who and where I am.

And then I signed back onto online dating and became hooked in the world of appearances. Swipe left for no, right for yes; how many yeses can I get? My ego went crazy, puffing up. *I'm attractive!* it screamed. And that's all fine and dandy in some ways, at least for a time. But a real relationship isn't about all that.

In April I watched Brené Brown's TED talk on authenticity and vulnerability. I was intent on owning my vulnerability. But then I got into online dating, and that type A part of my brain kicked in. *How can I win? I must win!* Now, you might think winning at online dating would be finding that one special someone. That's logical, right? Not to me. My brain said, winning is getting the most yeses; winning is getting the second date. Winning equals as much acceptance as you can find. And authenticity flew out the window. It's much easier to win if you read people well and act like a chameleon, changing yourself to who you think that person might want or need. I think I've always engaged in a little of that chameleoning.

So now, I try to show up and be real. Is it easy? No. There are a million articles and a hundred friends telling you how to play the game to win. All those games aren't about being real and authentic, though. I've found that the path to true happiness, true connection, is in being truly authentic and vulnerable, even when it's scary, even when it might hurt.

MARCH 15

Challenge

Identify one thing you often say or do to try to win approval from others. Then, make it a goal to not do this today so that you can focus less on what people think of you and more on simply *being* in their presence.

For Reflection

How frequently do you try to win approval when you're with other people?

How does it affect the way you act when you focus on other people's opinions?

How might it improve your interactions if you told yourself, and believed, that you have nothing to prove?

How Did It Go?

Were you able to focus less on other people's opinions of you? If so, how did you feel and act as a result, and how did this affect your interactions?

MARCH 16

Challenge

Watch Brené Brown's TED talk "The Power of Vulnerability" (http://tinybuddha.com/power-of-vulnerability) and then share the link with someone in your life who you believe could benefit from watching it.

For Reflection

Which part of Brené's talk inspired you the most?

Did you form any insights about yourself while watching this?

Who in your life might also benefit from watching this, and why?

How Did It Go?

Did the other person appreciate the video? Did it spark a valuable discussion?

MARCH 17

Challenge

Start your day by listening to a song that always empowers you to be your real self, and set the intention to show up authentically in your relationships.

Brainstorm: *For example, "Brave," by Sarah Bareilles, "Born This Way," by Lady Gaga, "Just the Way You Are" by Bruno Mars, or "Try" by Colbie Caillat.*

For Reflection

Do you usually set intentions at the start of your day? If so, how does this help and empower you?

How might it help to start your day with a song that inspires you to let your guard down and be authentic?

How Did It Go?

Did listening to this song at the start of your day empower you to be more genuine with others?

MARCH 18

Challenge

Write down one to three things you may be tempted to hide from other people, and for each, one reason why this is worth sharing—some way it makes you beautiful, has contributed to the person you've become, or may help other people. Read this list to yourself or out loud at every meal today.

1. I'm tempted to hide:

   This is worth sharing because:

2. I'm tempted to hide:

   This is worth sharing because:

3. I'm tempted to hide:

   This is worth sharing because:

How Did It Go?

Did this exercise help you see yourself differently, and act differently as a result?

MARCH 19

Challenge

Identify one adjective you'd use to describe yourself (not a role you hold, like "mother," "boyfriend," or your job title, and not something that's negative). Now, identify one specific way you could share this with someone in your life today.

Brainstorm: *For example, if you chose "intellectual," you could ask a friend to discuss a book you both read. Or, if you chose "fearless," you could ask a friend to join you in an adventure activity.*

For Reflection

Why did you choose this specific adjective?

Why do you value this part of your identity and enjoy sharing it with others?

How have you shared this with others in the past?

How Did It Go?

How did you decide to share this, and with whom? Was this rewarding for you, and why?

MARCH 20

Challenge

Ask someone a personal question about themselves that they can't answer with yes or no to start an authentic conversation.

For Reflection

What personal question do you think best allows someone to get to know someone else?

What question do you hope people ask you when you're first getting to know each other?

Why might someone appreciate you asking personal questions about their life?

How Did It Go?

Did asking a personal question facilitate a more authentic conversation than normal?

MARCH 21

Challenge

Think of one thing you regularly do because you think you'll better fit in, or at the very least, not stand out, and one thing you'd do if you were being true to yourself. Do the latter at some point today.

Brainstorm: *For example, if you regularly talk about things you think other people want to discuss, you could talk about your own interests instead. If you regularly force yourself to spend time in large groups, against your introverted nature, you could choose to spend time in a smaller group instead.*

For Reflection

Do you think it's important to fit in with others, and why?

What, if anything, do you fear you'll lose if you stand out?

What might you gain by being more authentic in those moments when you're tempted to blend?

How Did It Go?

What did you choose to do, and did you feel you were being truer to yourself than usual? Did your interactions with others feel more authentic and more rewarding as a result?

When given the chance, I would much rather bear pain on my own. It's incredibly difficult for me to be vulnerable and ask for help, or to share my pain with someone else. I think partly it's from my upbringing—living in the U.S., self-sufficiency is valued. We so often praise the individual who has done extraordinary things and see it as a sign of strength that they accomplished all of it on their own. I can understand that; it has led to independence and innovation. However, I'm also noticing a shift in understanding, of how we are all interconnected, and everything we do affects others.

A few years ago, while adjusting the volume on my cell phone, I tripped down the stairs. My ankle swelled up to the size of a grapefruit, and I had ugly purple and black bruises. I tore some ligaments and had a suspected fracture. Needless to say, I would not be running any marathons in the immediate future.

It was painful not only on a physical level, but also an emotional one. In my experience, being basically bedridden brought up all the issues I normally didn't have to face—one of those being humility. I couldn't walk, I couldn't do laundry because that required going down stairs, I couldn't grocery shop, I couldn't do anything but lie in my bed with my ankle propped on what seemed to be a thousand pillows.

As someone who prides herself on being independent, this was excruciating. The very last thing I *ever* wanted to do was ask for help, and there I was, needing it in a very big way.

Humility is not thinking I am inferior or superior to anyone else; it means understanding who I am and what I am capable of. When I sprained my ankle, I was incapable of doing things I used to take for granted. Instead of thinking in "should's" (i.e., I "should" be able to wash my dishes) humility allowed me to ask for help.

I had to swallow my pride. This meant admitting that not only was I unable to wash my dishes, but also admitting that someone else could. I called my dear friend, crying, because I had a sink full of dishes and couldn't stand long enough to clean them. She was happy to come over and wash them for me.

I think quite often in U.S. society there's an emphasis on *doing*. It's often advised that we get out there and help others, that we be of service, that we put aside our own troubles. But not much is talked about being the receiver. A friend of mine reminded me there are two parts to service: giving and receiving. That means somebody has to be on the receiving end. Somebody has to ask for help. Somebody has to say, "I can't do this alone."

I dream of a world where we all ask for help when we need it, physically, emotionally, or spiritually. A world where we understand that it's weakness, not strength, that binds us. A world where we see that true strength and humility is about knowing when to ask for help. A world where we understand that we were never meant to suffer through pain on our own. Because of my personal change and transformation, the ways I've learned humility, I know this world is possible.

MARCH 22

Challenge

Write down one to three beliefs you'd need to let go in order to ask someone else for help, and for each, one fact that disputes it.

Brainstorm: *For example, if you choose the belief "Asking for help is a sign of weakness," you could dispute that with "My mother asked me for help recently, and she's the strongest person I know." If you choose the belief, "People will think less of me if I ask for help," you could dispute that with, "My wife never thinks less of me when I ask her for help."*

1. Belief:

   Fact that disputes it:

2. Belief:

   Fact that disputes it:

3. Belief:

   Fact that disputes it:

How Did It Go?

Did you form any insights that may assist you in asking for help in the future?

MARCH 23

Challenge

Complete this sentence and tell it to someone in your life today: "You may not know this, but you really helped me by . . ."

For Reflection

Why was this person's action so helpful to you, and what has prevented you from sharing this with them in the past?

What may have happened (or not have happened) if this person hadn't helped you?

How does this one act represent your friend, colleague, or loved one as a person? Is this something you feel open to sharing with them?

How Did It Go?

Did the other person seem touched or surprised by what you shared with them?

MARCH 24

Challenge

Share a personal struggle with someone you trust, and ask for their help and advice.

For Reflection

When was the last time you asked someone for help with something going on in your personal life?

What, if anything, made asking for help hard for you, and was it worth it in the end?

If someone you knew was struggling, would you want them to ask *you* for help, and why?

How Did It Go?

How was this person able to help you? Do you think this strengthened your relationship?

MARCH 25

Challenge

Do something alone today, and smile at the people around you whenever you make eye contact.

Brainstorm: *Eat a meal at a restaurant alone, sit in the park drinking a coffee by yourself, or go to a movie you've wanted to see.*

For Reflection

Do you feel comfortable doing things in public alone? Why or why not?

When you've been alone in public in the past, have you tried to avoid connection with strangers? If so, why?

When you see other people alone in public, what do you assume about them? If you form negative assumptions, what's a more positive way to interpret their choice to spend time alone?

How Did It Go?

What did you do alone, and how did this feel? Did you connect with anyone around you?

MARCH 26

Challenge

Identify someone you'd like to form a deeper relationship with, romantically or platonically, and ask if they'd like to get together, just the two of you.

For Reflection

When you're not close with someone but would like to be, do you usually wait for them to initiate plans?

What fears, if any, prevent you from inviting them out? Is it possible that others have the same fears and would appreciate you acting in spite of yours?

What's the best thing that could happen if you invited this particular person out?

How Did It Go?

What did you invite the other person to do, and did they accept your invitation? Did you learn anything from this experience that will help you take initiative in the future?

MARCH 27

Challenge

Complete this sentence: "I'm tired of pretending that . . ." Now identify one specific thing you can do to stop pretending today—and do it.

Brainstorm: *For example, if you frequently pretend you have everything "together," you could tell someone about the things you think you're failing at. If you frequently pretend that you're not sensitive, you could share your feelings with a loved one and even cry in front of them.*

For Reflection

Why do you think you pretend in this way?

How does it hurt you to do this?

What's the best thing that could happen if you stopped pretending?

How Did It Go?

How did you feel when doing this thing? Did you feel tempted to pretend? Were you able to act authentically instead?

MARCH 28

Challenge

Share a thought, belief, or opinion that you're nervous to share, and do so in a public setting, whether it's in a meeting at work or at a dinner with friends.

For Reflection

How often do you withhold your thoughts, beliefs, and opinions for fear of being judged or rejected?

How does it limit your potential for connection when you withhold what you really think and feel?

Would you feel more comfortable voicing your thoughts and beliefs if you considered that this could lead you to people who appreciate what you have to say?

How Did It Go?

How did you feel facing this fear? What happened as a result?

MARCH 29

Challenge

Say "I love you" to someone you love but rarely tell.

For Reflection

Do you feel comfortable telling people you love them? If not, in which relationships do you feel most uncomfortable, and why?

How do you feel when someone says "I love you" to you?

What do you think you'd regret more at the end of your life: saying I love you and feeling vulnerable, or never having said it at all?

How Did It Go?

To whom did you say "I love you"? Are you glad you did? Why or why not?

MARCH 30

Challenge

If you usually wear makeup, snap a makeup-free selfie and text it to a friend. If you don't usually wear makeup, or if you'd prefer a different challenge, share an embarrassing story, something that you'd find funny if you weren't taking yourself too seriously.

For Reflection

How do you feel about being seen when you haven't put time into your appearance?

How do you think controlling how people see you creates a sense of separation?

Why do you appreciate when your friends feel comfortable enough to be seen in their natural state?

How Did It Go?

Which challenge did you choose? Did this feel liberating? Why or why not?

MARCH 31

Challenge

When you'd like to text or e-mail someone today to keep the exchange easy, call instead; or, even better, say it face-to-face.

For Reflection

How often do you send texts to keep exchanges quick and easy, and why?

How does it limit your potential for connection to communicate in this way?

How and why might it strengthen your relationships to make the extra effort?

How Did It Go?

Did you feel like you had a more meaningful conversation by having it over the phone or in person?

MONTHLY REVIEW

- Which challenges were the most helpful for you, and why?
- Which challenges were the most difficult for you, and why?
- What did you learn about yourself through the process of completing these challenges? Did you form any new insights about being authentic and vulnerable?
- What did you learn about the people in your life?
- Did these challenges strengthen your relationships, and how?
- Did you identify any areas for improvement and growth?
- Head over to http://tinybuddha.com/love-forums to share your experiences with other readers!

APRIL

Releasing Anger and Forgiving

Reflections from CLORIS KYLIE

When my husband had an affair, I directed all my anger at the "other woman," who contacted me to tell me I was wasting my time by trying to save my marriage. She became aggressive and even created a public scene worthy of *Jerry Springer*. As my resentment grew, so did my inability to find inner peace.

I sought sources of inspiration to help me forgive, but the answer didn't come from a book. Instead, it came from three amazing, brave people who chose to forgive when anyone else would have thought it impossible.

First, I met a woman who had been confined to a wheelchair after a brutal attack and yet decided to forgive her attacker to free herself from the role of victim. Next, I met a woman whose family had been killed in the Rwandan genocide. Instead of hating the murderers, she found room in her heart to forgive them and started a campaign advocating love and tolerance among children in the school systems that has taken her all over the world. Finally, I met the mother of a six-year-old who was murdered in an elementary-school shooting. Instead of wallowing in resentment after the horrific tragedy, she created a foundation to teach and foster love in the school systems.

Meeting these three women illuminated my path to forgiveness. I forgave the "other woman" for her behavior. I could see that she thought she was doing what was best for her at the time. I also forgave myself for the anger and resentment I had experienced. Two weeks after I made the decision to forgive, I was grocery shopping when I felt a tap on my shoulder. It was the "other woman." My stomach sank. Was she going to try to hurt me again?

"I wasn't sure whether to approach you or not," she said. "But I wanted to apologize for what I did. It wasn't right and you didn't deserve it. I'm sorry."

Coincidence? I choose to see what happened as proof that forgiveness not only allows love to flow back into our own hearts, but also to fill the hearts of those who've hurt us.

Reflections from GLORIA ECHEVERRY MARTINEZ

Five years ago, I felt as if I lost my entire life when my husband died from brain cancer at only twenty-nine years of age. I was incredibly angry, bitter, and full of hate. I lashed out at the ones I loved, pushed people away, completely isolated myself, and drank way too much.

Somehow, one of my friends pushed his way into my complicated mess of a life and convinced me to take a walk with him. He assured me that it would clear my mind and make me feel better, and it actually did. It released a lot of stress and anger. It became my new outlet, my therapy. Anytime I felt stressed or angry, I would just walk. Sometimes twenty minutes, sometimes an hour, then it progressed into a more vigorous exercise routine that I still religiously keep up with today.

In the midst of all the walking and working out, I also danced, meditated, became more spiritual, and eventually stopped drinking for further healing, clarity, acceptance, and a more positive perspective on life. My parents also bought me a puppy, and he has helped me tremendously just by being present.

Through all of my healing, I've accepted my husband's death and I've fought to become a better person, because I know that's what he would want for me. The anger still surfaces every now and then, but now I have many outlets that help me deal with it in a healthier, more mindful way. These outlets have taught me to turn negativity into positivity, and that is what I do with anger. I release it into love and forgiveness.

APRIL 1

Challenge

Use the "countdown technique" whenever you're angry today. Before saying or doing anything, count down from twenty to gain a sense of composure.

For Reflection

Have you ever responded quickly and impulsively in anger and then regretted it?

What thoughts, beliefs, and fears often cause this knee-jerk reaction?

How does it affect your relationships when you react this way, and does it ever help the situation?

How Did It Go?

Did pausing help you challenge your initial reaction? Did you avoid saying something you may have regretted later?

APRIL 2

Challenge

Clean a room in your home, and as you do this, visualize yourself cleaning your mind of all the anger you feel toward someone.

For Reflection

Toward whom are you currently harboring anger, and why?

How much space is this anger taking up in your mind?

What would your life be like without this anger?

How Did It Go?

Did it help you to combine visualization with a physical act of release? If so, do you think this affected your interactions with others?

APRIL 3

Challenge

Think about how your parents (or the people who raised you) processed and responded to anger. Write down anything unhealthy you learned from them and what might be a healthier choice. (The goal is not to blame them for their shortcomings, but to recognize how you formed some of your patterns and what can do to change them.)

Unhealthy behavior:

Healthier choice:

Unhealthy behavior:

Healthier choice:

Unhealthy behavior:

Healthier choice:

How Did It Go?

Did you form any new insights about how you process and respond to anger? How might these help you going forward?

APRIL 4

Challenge

Set aside at least ten minutes for aerobic exercise today. Exercising releases endorphins, reduces stress, and works off excess energy—and it's a great way to release pent-up anger.

Brainstorm: *If you don't have time for a full workout, it could be something simple, like doing jumping jacks or dancing in your living room.*

For Reflection

How does exercising usually affect your state of mind?

Has exercising ever helped you clear your head and find a constructive solution to a problem?

How Did It Go?

Did you feel any different after exercising? Did this affect how you engaged with others?

APRIL 5

Challenge

Every time you dwell on a hurtful past experience today, put something heavy in your pocket, purse, or backpack. Feel how these items weigh you down, and then, as you remove each one at the end of the day, think, *I am letting go of my pain and anger so I can be light and free.*

For Reflection

Which painful stories from your past do you regularly dwell on or rehash?

What are you hoping to accomplish in dwelling or rehashing these stories—and does it actually help you?

How do these stories from the past weigh you down and keep you from feeling free in the present?

How Did It Go?

How many things did you accumulate by the end of the day? Could you feel the physical weight lift as you removed them? How about the emotional weight?

APRIL 6

Challenge

If/when you think a self-victimizing thought today, like *Why do bad things always happen to me?*, tell yourself something empowering, such as, *I may have been hurt in the past, and I have every right to be angry, but I can choose to heal and deal with my anger constructively in the present.*

For Reflection

Have you ever gotten stuck in a victim mind-set because of things that happened to you?

How might it have changed your perspective to consider that things happen *for* you, not to you—that you learn, grow, and develop new strengths through every hardship you endure?

Can you think of anyone who could easily have stayed stuck in a victim mind-set but instead turned adversity into an opportunity?

How Did It Go?

How many self-victimizing thoughts did you catch, and were you able to change your perspective? If so, did you feel more empowered as a result?

APRIL 7

Challenge

Set aside a few minutes for progressive relaxation today. Lie down, and then starting with your feet, tense and relax each body part, working your way up to your head. Relaxing your muscles will help you release anger from your body and create a sense of inner calm to bring into your interactions.

Brainstorm: *Perhaps you can carve out this time on a lunch break or right before you go to bed.*

For Reflection

How do you feel physically when you're angry? Where specifically do you often feel anger in your body?

What other emotions pop up when you feel physically tense, and how does that affect your demeanor?

How does it affect your mental state when you release tension in your body?

How Did It Go?

How did you feel before the progressive relaxation, and how did you feel after? Do you think this exercise had any effect on your interactions with others?

When I was a teenager, my parents fought all the time and constantly threatened divorce. At sixteen I stopped eating for three months. That was the beginning of a tumultuous relationship with my mother, who wasn't willing or able to look at what was happening at home as a trigger for my challenges.

Together with physical discipline, controlling behavior, and constant grounding even into my late teens, I spun into bouts of anxiety, depression, a period of agoraphobia, anger, bitterness, and resentment.

In my thirties it became evident that my mother was changing and really wanted a relationship with me. She couldn't see why our relationship was the way it was. It was pretty obvious to me, but she had no idea. She wasn't equipped with the awareness to see it or to take responsibility for her actions. Nevertheless, as the years went on I saw my mother being a much kinder, more loving person. Her old habits and behaviors seemed to melt away. Perhaps having distance between us helped (thousands of miles). I yearned for a relationship with her. I saw my friends had wonderful relationships with their mothers and felt I was missing out.

The turning point came when I chose to see her differently. I looked at what my resentment and bitterness were doing to me—fueling my anger and depression and denying me a relationship with my mother. I recognized that I had also played my part in our relationship, and that I could take responsibility for that. I saw her as a fallible human being with her own fears and anxiety and found compassion for her and her situation back then. I was able to forgive her.

No conversation was had. She wasn't able to. So I let go of the need to have her begging for my forgiveness. In doing this, I found peace, and we had a very close relationship for five years after that. Then she died suddenly. I'm glad to say I'm able to look back with no regrets. The experience I had with her in the early years is a distant memory and not something I think about. I now have my memories of love and joy in those final years with my mother. And the gift of that experience has inspired me to help others experience deep inner and outer healing too. I am deeply blessed.

My father was a practitioner of traditional Chinese medicine (TCM). When my mother became pregnant with me, he attempted an herbal abortion (most likely involving a toxic abortifacient). As a result, I was born with numerous congenital defects. Subsequently, my parents entered negotiations to sell me to a childless couple. I was already contending with teen angst when I learned these dark secrets.

For over twenty years, I unconsciously suppressed my emotional pain, but acted out by stepping up my involvement with gangs and by gambling. I also suffered recurring nightmares—of being poisoned in utero, and of being forcibly handed over to strange people. Years of psychotherapy provided insight and short-term relief occasionally, but my self-perception of being "unwanted" and a burden was ingrained. Numerous therapists encouraged me to forgive my parents, but every attempt I made felt disingenuous.

I began practicing mindfulness meditation to calm my mind and discovered many additional benefits. This motivated me to adopt a spiritual practice, which awakened the love and kindness that had been buried inside of me. Eventually, this enabled me to transform the anger toward my parents into compassion and empathy for them. During one meditation session, I felt my mother and father's terror when they were confronted with the pregnancy. I recognized that my parents were barely able to provide for themselves and my four older siblings.

Studying the doctrine of "no self" helped me to discern that the attempted abortion was not personal. Their fear prevented any attachment to the fetus. Through meditation, I also gained insight into my parents' decision to sell me. I was finally able to acknowledge and accept that their motivation was to secure a better future for me. It was, in essence, an act of love.

My spiritual awakening opened my heart, empowering me to forgive my mother and father. I continually pray that they are both resting in peace.

APRIL 8

Challenge

Write down how you wish other people would respond when angry with you—what they'd say or do, or not say or do. Now make it a goal to act in this way toward others who may anger you today.

When people are angry with me, I'd like them to respond by:

How Did It Go?

Were you able to respond to others, when angry, in the way you'd like them to respond to you?

APRIL 9

Challenge

Visualize everyone you meet today as a young child who is doing his or her best, making mistakes, and hoping for your understanding and forgiveness. Keep this in mind when choosing how to respond to missteps.

For Reflection

When a child angers you, do you respond differently than you respond to adults? If so, why do you think this is?

What specifically do you do differently?

What would you need to believe to offer this same understanding and compassion to adults?

How Did It Go?

Did this visualization exercise help you treat people with more understanding and forgiveness? If so, how did it benefit you to act with less anger and more compassion?

APRIL 10

Challenge

Search YouTube for "Free guided meditation for forgiveness" and choose one to listen to, while sitting comfortably or lying down.

For Reflection

Have you ever felt anger so intense that it almost seemed like a past event was repeating itself in the present?

Did you feel as though this was involuntary—that you had no choice but to think those thoughts, see those images, and feel those feelings?

If you knew meditation was the key to feeling present and free from the past, would you make the time to do it more regularly?

How Did It Go?

How did you feel after listening to the guided meditation? Did it help calm your thoughts? Might it benefit you to do this regularly going forward?

APRIL 11

Challenge

Place this quote by Robert Brault somewhere you'll see it throughout the day, to help yourself forgive without needing to hear the words *I'm sorry:* *"Life becomes easier when you learn to accept an apology you never got."*

For Reflection

Do you find it easier to let go and forgive when someone apologizes?

Have you ever had a hard time owning up to pain you caused someone else? If so, why?

What pain do you think someone may be trying to avoid by not acknowledging the pain they've caused—and does it help at all to empathize with this instinct to avoid pain?

How Did It Go?

Did this exercise improve your ability to let go, even if just for a while?

APRIL 12

Challenge

Identify something negative you believe about yourself because of a past mistake for which you've struggled to forgive yourself (for example, "I'm a bad person")—something that is *not* a fact, even if it may feel like one. Look for one piece of proof to support the opposite belief today. (For example, helping your sister could be proof that you are, in fact, a good person.)

For Reflection

What "proof" from your past have you used to back up this negative belief about yourself?

How has this negative belief limited or hurt you?

What would your closest loved one say if you told them that you hold this belief about yourself?

How Did It Go?

What proof did you find to support the opposite belief? Did this help you forgive yourself?

APRIL 13

Challenge

Think of a painful event that led you to feel angry with someone and hesitant to offer forgiveness. Now write down all the ways you may have contributed to this event to help decrease your anger toward the other person.

Painful Event:

How you may have contributed to it:

What you could have done differently (in the situation or in responding to it):

How Did It Go?

Did it soften your anger to recognize that you've *both* made mistakes?

APRIL 14

Challenge

Label a jar or box with the words *Small Stuff*. Whenever you're feeling annoyed by something that isn't really a big deal, write it on a piece of paper and put it in the box or jar. At the end of the day, shred or burn these as an act of release.

For Reflection

What types of "little things" do you sometimes overreact about?

Why do you think these things trigger such anger in you?

Are there any big issues that you need to address so that these little things don't trigger you in this way?

How Did It Go?

Did this activity help you let go of "small stuff" that may otherwise have upset you? How did this affect your interactions with others?

For most of my adolescent and adult life, I have been easily angered. I coined the problem I was having as "perceived threat syndrome" where I saw threats all around me and reacted unnecessarily with a fight-or-flight response. Of course, I believed I knew why I was doing this. During my youth I was bullied relentlessly and had built up anger and low self-confidence as a result.

My anger persisted in adulthood because I had yet to forgive these past bullies, who I saw as my demons, and hadn't learned to let go of the past. Eventually, I knew it was time to do something about this, and I knew social media could help.

My first bully growing up was a guy I'll call Bob. To me, he was the evil person I remembered from childhood, over thirty-five years ago. I needed closure; I needed to try to reach him and see the human inside of the demon I had created. So I went on Facebook and in about two minutes found and contacted him.

Bob sent me his phone number and I called. I told him he was my childhood bully and I wanted to change my memory of him and forgive him. He immediately started apologizing and telling me of the abuse he dealt with at home during his childhood. We talked for an hour and found that, as adults, we were more similar than different. Just as I learned, you must find a way to let go of the past to release anger and resentment, whether you find the person as I did or work through it by journaling or talking to someone you trust. You can't change the past. All you can do is live for today and find peace in the present—and that starts with forgiveness.

When my good friend moved out of the apartment we shared, in her place came a new roommate, who was no picnic to be around. She was angry at the world, surrounded by toxic relationships, and altogether a mess. She kept my other roommates and me up with her partying and loud phone calls well into the night.

After a short time of living together, sleep deprivation and frustration kicked in, leading me to take her aside and share my concerns. She apologized and promised to make an effort with her actions. Pleased with myself for confronting the issue head-on, I expected a change. To my surprise, less than one week later, she was back to her old ways. Then my frustration and anger intensified and began to take a toll on my health and overall wellness.

I felt helpless after the earlier conversation had failed and believed that I was out of options. A few weeks later, I walked into the apartment while she was in the middle of one of her fits. In that moment, the usual frustration and anger I felt toward her dissipated and were replaced with pity. I then realized that the way she chose to live her life, full of anger, mistrust, and bitterness, led her to the sad and lonely place that she was in today. I realized I could still change my reaction, and the frustration and anger that accompanied it; otherwise, I would end up like her, bitter and alone.

I was not as helpless as I felt and I had the power to change the situation—if I let go of my bitterness and focused on finding a solution. After that, I saw things from a new perspective and eventually got a new roommate. We all have the power to let go of things. By letting go, we release the anger that keeps us stuck and allow ourselves the freedom to see our options.

APRIL 15

Challenge

Make "don't take it personally" your mantra today. If anyone seems excessively angry with you, consider that you merely triggered some deeper pain, and then choose to respond calmly and compassionately.

For Reflection

Have you ever lashed out at someone and later realized it wasn't really (or at least not fully) about them; it was about something else below the surface?

Did that person respond to your anger with anger, and how did the situation escalate as a result?

How would you want someone to respond if you were unknowingly acting on misdirected anger?

How Did It Go?

Were there any situations you were tempted to take personally today? Did this mantra help you respond differently than you would have otherwise?

APRIL 16

Challenge

Communicate to someone why you're feeling angry, with the intent of reaching an amicable resolution, using "I feel" language. So, instead of saying, "You always cancel last minute," say, "When you cancel last minute, I feel like I'm not important to you."

For Reflection

When you've blamed others in the past, how have they responded?

Has this helped address or solve the real issue?

How do you respond when blamed—and how might you respond if someone expressed how your actions affect them, instead?

How Did It Go?

Did the other person seem open to your feelings? Did this conversation go differently than those that involved blaming?

APRIL 17

Challenge

Write "Only Human Card" on an index card and carry it in your purse or pocket. Whenever someone irritates you today, remember they too are only human—they hold the same card—and silently forgive them for whatever they did that bothered you.

For Reflection

Do you ever hold others to higher standards than you could actually live up to?

Which of your own expectations would you struggle to consistently meet?

How might it benefit your relationships to loosen your grip on these?

How Did It Go?

Did this exercise help you release your expectations and cut others slack? Do you think you made a positive difference in anyone's day by remembering we're all only human?

APRIL 18

Challenge

Identify something hurtful you've done for which you haven't forgiven yourself. Then apologize to the person you hurt both to ease their pain and to pave the way for self-forgiveness.

For Reflection

Why have you been hard on yourself for hurting this person? Did you intend to hurt them, and if so, why?

How have you hurt *yourself* in denying yourself forgiveness?

Why do you believe this person deserves an apology from you—and what is one reason you deserve forgiveness, in spite of what you did?

How Did It Go?

How did the person respond to your apology? Did this make it any easier to forgive yourself?

APRIL 19

Challenge

Agree to disagree with someone today instead of getting angry and fighting for them to see things your way.

For Reflection

When someone doesn't see things your way, does it ever help to angrily tell them why they're wrong?

How do you feel when others get angry with you for having a different perspective?

What's more important for your relationships—that you always agree, or that you respect each other's points of view?

How Did It Go?

About what did you agree to disagree? How do you think it benefited your relationship to do this?

APRIL 20

Challenge

Whenever you're feeling angry with or threatened by someone today, touch one or two fingers to your lips. According to Rick Hanson, author of *Buddha's Brain,* this stimulates your parasympathetic nervous system, which creates a feeling of calm and relaxation and pulls you out of fight-or-flight mode. It will also force you to pause before you react.

For Reflection

Have you ever felt a panicked fight-or-flight response when confronted with something that wasn't actually a major threat to your well-being?

Did you respond in a way that you wish you didn't, in retrospect?

How does this state of high alert affect your ability to respond rationally and calmly?

How Did It Go?

Did this exercise calm you? How did you respond as a result? Do you think you prevented a bad situation from getting worse?

APRIL 21

Challenge

Make today a no-sarcasm day. Instead of expressing your anger, frustration, or annoyance sarcastically, be clear and direct.

For Reflection

Have you ever used sarcasm to avoid directly expressing your anger?

What fears do you think have caused you to avoid expressing your anger clearly?

How does it affect your relationships when you use sarcasm in this way—and how might it improve your relationships to be more direct?

How Did It Go?

Was it hard not to react sarcastically today? Did you resolve any issues by being clear and direct that may otherwise have gone unresolved?

All my romantic relationships have ended quickly and painfully. I often compared the new men in my life to the old ones. From my former boyfriends' mistakes, I always found a reason to walk away from the current one. I even occasionally returned to old boyfriends in hopes that things would change, but they never did. Over time, the anger of past injustices reappeared many times, and I couldn't overcome it.

A few years ago, I decided to make a change for myself. I stopped communication with all my exes to rid the poison I thought they brought to my life. At first it was liberating, but soon the old feelings of regret and pain came back. I couldn't stop being the victim and feeling hurt for what was done to me. I finally understood that the only way to truly be free from anger was through forgiveness.

This year, I started writing letters to each of the men whom I'd loved and then hated for so long. I told them my feelings, good and bad, and apologized for the part I played in ending each relationship. Lastly, I forgave them for the mistakes they made—the mistakes that haunted me for years. I sealed each letter with a wish for their happiness and a kiss. I have never felt more content and free than when I placed those letters in the mail. It gave me the resolution that I needed, to say what my heart felt in its entirety and let go.

As I finished sending the last letter, I knew that my heart was ready to love without the burden of past misfortune. I can finally give myself completely to love without excuses or being a victim.

I met my ex-boyfriend while we were both in recovery for alcoholism. We dated for a few months until he relapsed. There were always two voices in the back of my head: one telling me this relationship wasn't healthy and I needed to walk away, and the other telling me to stick it out. That second voice told me I could lead by example, that if he could only see how I was improving my life by being sober, he would do the same.

I kept holding on tighter, afraid he would leave and that I wasn't good enough. When he did leave, abruptly, I was devastated. I expected him to fill that void that was still inside me, despite all the work I was doing on myself. My codependency flared up in all sorts of unhealthy ways: stalking Facebook, obsessing over what I could have said or done to make him stay, resting all my self-worth on his opinion of me. I was against feeling anger toward him because I felt I deserved to be treated this way.

With time, a network of support, and my higher power, I went back to the basics of my program: one day at a time. Each day was a struggle, redirecting my thoughts from negative/obsessive to reflective/self-loving. Eventually, I acknowledged and felt my anger and could let him go. When I find myself wanting to check on him or obsess, I redirect my thinking to my progress and what I could do with this experience to help others. I choose not to hold on to the negativity of that relationship but the self-awareness and love I've cultivated thus far in myself.

Today, I thank him for leaving. What I've learned by feeling and releasing my anger and choosing to forgive is that people come in and out of our lives every day, and they all teach us something about ourselves. If we're open-minded, we can reap the benefits and in turn, help others.

APRIL 22

Challenge

On a separate piece of paper, write a letter of forgiveness to someone toward whom you've felt bitter and angry (to send or to burn as an act of release).

For Reflection

What are some things you've wanted to tell this person about their actions and how they affected you?

What's prevented you from sharing these things in the past?

If you'd like to maintain a relationship with this person, what, if anything, do you need from them to do that?

How Did It Go?

Was this a cathartic experience for you? Did you decide to send or burn the letter?

APRIL 23

Challenge

Identify one way you can help others using a lesson you learned from a painful past relationship. Then put it into practice and help someone with this today.

Brainstorm: *For example, if you learned not to lose yourself in a relationship, you could invite a friend who seems to have lost herself to join you in doing something you know she loves. Or you could write a blog post sharing your experience and lesson.*

For Reflection

When a relationship ends, do you usually try to identify lessons to help you going forward?

How does it help you (or how do you think it *would* help you) to focus on lessons learned when reflecting on a painful relationship?

How do you feel knowing that your past pain can actually make a positive difference in someone else's life?

How Did It Go?

How did you use your lesson to help someone else today, and how do you think it benefited them?

APRIL 24

Challenge

Identify an anger trigger within one of your relationships, and why this particular behavior triggers you in this way. Then identify how you can change this or change your response to it—and do this today.

Brainstorm: *For example, it may trigger your anger when your partner doesn't do his share of the housework because you feel this is unfair. You could change this by asking him to do specific tasks around the house, or change your response to it by reminding yourself,* I may do more around the house, but he does more in other areas of our relationship. He isn't wronging me, so I can let that story go.

For Reflection

What do you usually think when this person does this thing?

How do these thoughts keep you angry and stuck?

How do you act as a result of these thoughts, and how does this affect your relationship?

How Did It Go?

Did you change the situation or your response? Did you feel better about your relationship and avoid unnecessary conflict as a result?

APRIL 25

Challenge

As an exercise to put things in perspective, go about your day as if you were going to die tomorrow. Whenever you feel angry with someone, ask yourself, *Would I want to spend my last day alive dwelling on this?*

For Reflection

What type of things have you dwelled on lately that you'd be more willing to let go if you knew it was your last day on Earth?

What has caused you to dwell on these things?

What would you tell yourself to help let them go if you knew your time with your loved ones was almost up?

How Did It Go?

Did this shift in perspective help you? If so, what kinds of things did you let go, and why were they not worth dwelling on?

APRIL 26

Challenge

Identify someone toward whom you've felt resentment for not meeting an unexpressed expectation. Share this expectation with them today so they can better understand and meet your need—or they can explain why they can't.

For Reflection

Has anyone ever felt annoyed with you for not meeting an expectation that they never shared?

Would you have at least tried to meet this expectation if they had shared it with you?

What, if anything, prevents you from sharing your expectations with people, and what could you do to overcome this?

How Did It Go?

What expectation did you share, and how did this benefit you and your relationship?

APRIL 27

Challenge

Imagine that you are the hero in a movie, and all the pain you've experienced has helped you grow, and will eventually help you thrive in life. Give that movie a title and write it on a piece of paper to carry in your purse or pocket. Look at this whenever you're feeling angry or hurt today to remind yourself that you are the hero of your story, not the victim.

For Reflection

Why did you choose this particular title for the movie of your life?

If your life were a movie, what would be the main lesson that you, as the hero, needed to learn?

How might that lesson help you thrive in life?

How Did It Go?

Did it soften your anger to realize you're not a victim, and to consider pain valuable to your growth?

APRIL 28

Challenge

Create a sense of safety in an unhealthy relationship by setting a boundary.

Brainstorm: *For example, decide to reduce or cut off contact with someone who regularly hurts you, or to leave the room whenever a particular topic comes up.*

For Reflection

What fears, if any, have prevented you from setting and enforcing boundaries in the past?

When you've struggled with setting boundaries, how has it affected your relationships and/or caused you pain?

How might your relationships improve if you got clearer about your boundaries and took responsibility for enforcing them?

How Did It Go?

What boundary did you set? Did this help you in any way, and how might it help you going forward?

APRIL 29

Challenge

Listen to peaceful music in your car and practice deep breathing to help minimize road rage, or identify some other way you can make your drive (or commute) less stressful and more enjoyable.

For Reflection

What types of things do you think and feel when you're stuck in traffic?

How do other drivers affect you when they're lost in road rage, and how do you think you affect the other drivers when you let anger, stress, or anxiety take over?

What are some other things you could do to make your drive or commute less stressful and more enjoyable?

How Did It Go?

Did you feel any calmer on the road, and were you less annoyed with other drivers? Was your drive more enjoyable?

APRIL 30

Challenge

Share with an unbiased outsider why you're angry with another person. Then, ask them what they think or see as an impartial observer that may help you let go of your anger and forgive.

For Reflection

Can you think of a time when someone was angry and you saw things differently, as an impartial observer?

How might it have benefited that person to see things from your perspective and act accordingly?

What thoughts or beliefs would you need to let go in order to adopt a new perspective?

How Did It Go?

What did the other person share with you? Did this help you change your perspective, let go of your anger, and forgive?

MONTHLY REVIEW

- Which challenges were the most helpful for you, and why?
- Which challenges were the most difficult for you, and why?
- What did you learn about yourself through the process of completing these challenges? Did you form any new insights about releasing anger and forgiving those who hurt you?
- What did you learn about the people in your life?
- Did these challenges strengthen your relationships, and how?
- Did you identify any areas for improvement and growth?
- Head over to http://tinybuddha.com/love-forums to share your experiences with other readers!

MAY

Attention and Listening

Reflections from ALANA MBANZA

The silence was deafening on the phone. I had to break it before it stretched on forever.

"Are you still there?"

I knew he was, of course. He responded by saying he wanted to see how long the silence would last.

"It makes me uncomfortable."

I immediately wished I hadn't said that. I wondered what triggered the statement, why I felt the need to express my discomfort. When he asked the obvious "why," another unanticipated response flew out of my mouth.

"I feel like you're not listening to me."

I quickly attempted to laugh it off and carried on with the conversation. But the encounter stuck with me and showed up in my daily journaling.

Intellectually, I knew he had *heard* me. There was no reason why he wouldn't have. The sounds I made traveled through space and were received by his eardrums. But feeling like I'm being *listened to* involves some degree of validation. I need to know that my thoughts, feelings, and ideas are being understood and accepted.

Prior to the prolonged silence, I shared some things that left me feeling pretty vulnerable. I was wide open. This is not a feeling I enjoy or find comfort in, so in the space of silence my insecurities became almost unbearable. This has happened many times before in other conversations with other people. If I share authentically and vulnerably, I need the other person to respond in a certain way or I start to feel neurotic. It had nothing to do with him, and everything to do with the difficulty of accepting my own feelings.

I read somewhere that women tend to qualify our statements more than men. Built into our approach to communication is the implicit belief that what we say isn't valid in its own right. We need tacit approval from others. An innate desire to maintain harmonious relationships has been twisted by social conventions into a tendency to seek external stamps of approval for everything we say. But when we look to others too much, we relinquish our personal power and put others into the role of "approver." This sets us up for power games, frustration, disappointment, and unhappiness.

While we want to participate in conversations that include true connection and deep listening, it serves no one to give our power away. We need to learn to listen to each other and reflect in a way that lets others know we are listening, without depending on them for validation.

Keep your power intact and become a better communicator by deeply listening in conversations. Trust in your truth and self-worth so you don't need to seek validation from others. Learn to embrace silence as an opportunity to receive. And clearly communicate what you need from others, without expecting them to respond in a particular way. True communication requires the ability to receive others' authentic expression, even if they don't say what you want to hear, while having the courage to share yourself spontaneously and authentically.

MAY 1

Challenge

Practice active listening today. Whenever someone shares their feelings with you, repeat back to them what you heard, in your own words, to let them know you understand.

For Reflection

Have you ever felt like someone heard you but didn't really understand?

How would it have made a difference for you if you knew they truly got what you were saying?

Do you find it easy to focus when other people share their feelings? If not, what gets in the way, and how can you overcome this?

How Did It Go?

Did people seem to appreciate that you made the effort to listen fully and understand them?

MAY 2

Challenge

Before you share your thoughts and feelings today, take a moment to silently repeat this mantra: "My goal is to be honest, not to control how other people receive my honesty."

For Reflection

Do you frequently look to other people to validate your thoughts and feelings?

If yes, why do you believe your thoughts and feelings aren't valid in their own right?

What would you need to believe about yourself to own your thoughts and feelings, whether others validate them or not?

How Did It Go?

Did you feel more secure in sharing your feelings, and less dependent on a specific response? How did this affect your interactions?

MAY 3

Challenge

Take a day of silence. Enjoy silent activities, like walking, reading, or listening to music, and focus on the sounds in your environment to strengthen your listening skills. If today is a workday for you, commit to remaining silent for a small window of time, before or after work.

Tip: *You may want to keep a pen and paper nearby, in case you need to communicate or jot down any fears or worries that might make it noisy in your head.*

For Reflection

Have you ever remained silent for a prolonged period of time? If so, did you gain anything through this experience?

Does the thought of remaining silent for a full day or a portion of the day feel daunting to you? If so, why?

What obstacles do you think you might encounter, and how can you plan in advance to overcome them?

How Did It Go?

Did you remain silent for the whole day, or a small window of time? How did you feel after? Did you feel more present?

MAY 4

Challenge

Think about what goes through your mind when you really need to talk but instead of listening, the other person continually interjects with stories and problems of their own. Write below how this makes you feel and keep this in mind today as a reminder to listen fully when other people need an ear instead of making things about you.

How Did It Go?

Did this exercise change how you listened and responded to others today?

MAY 5

Challenge

Meditate for five to twenty minutes or take a short walk so you can listen to your intuition about whatever is currently causing you stress or pain.

Brainstorm: *You could do this on your lunch break, or you could turn a nighttime bath into a meditative experience.*

For Reflection

Have you ever had a gut feeling and ignored it only to later wish you hadn't?

If so, what prevented you from following your intuition?

How might your life improve if you always listened to your intuition and acted on what you learned?

How Did It Go?

What message did your intuition have for you, and what can do today to act on it?

MAY 6

Challenge

Start a conversation with someone who has a different opinion than you so you can practice listening and understanding another's point of view when you don't agree with it. Resist the temptation to argue or debate them.

For Reflection

How do you usually respond—in words and body language—when someone expresses an opinion that you don't agree with?

Do you feel a need to change their mind, and if so, why?

What would you need to let go to simply hear them out, without turning the conversation into a debate?

How Did It Go?

Were you able to listen without arguing? Did you feel the urge to change their mind, and if so, why?

MAY 7

Challenge

Do a "needs scavenger hunt" today. Pay attention to those around you and identify three types of people: someone who seems to need recognition, someone who needs encouragement, and someone who needs empathy. Then offer these things to them.

For Reflection

What are some things you've identified as signs that someone needs recognition?

What are some things you've identified as signs that someone needs encouragement?

What are some things you've identified as signs that someone needs empathy?

How Did It Go?

Did you pay closer attention to the people around you as a result of this challenge? Were you able to recognize people who needed these things, and if so, how did you provide recognition, encouragement, and empathy?

Reflections from JILL DAHL

I used to take pride in being the problem solver among my friends. I knew they could call me with their relationship dilemmas, parental woes, or work issues, and I would help them find a practical solution.

One day a few years ago, my dear friend Esther and I decided to take her three children for an after-dinner walk. While they played at a park, Esther confided to me that she was really overwhelmed that week, as she was juggling some significant work and family obligations.

I immediately went into problem-solver mode, peppering her with questions to determine her biggest sources of frustration, and asking what she had tried so far to address the issue. On the verge of tears she blurted out, "I just need you to listen to me right now, not fix it!"

I felt my throat get tight and tears well up in my eyes. Looking back, I now realize that her response triggered an intense feeling of shame—I felt that I was a horrible friend for being overly analytical instead of simply expressing empathy.

"I'm so sorry," I whispered hoarsely. "You're right. I wasn't really listening, I was just trying to fix it."

Esther slipped her arm around me and put her head on my shoulder.

"I forgive you," she said. "I know you were just trying to help. I just *really* needed you to listen instead of jumping in with a solution."

That day I made a vow to myself that I would put aside my fix-it mind-set and make sure that I was truly listening when a friend shared her problems. Instead of asking questions to determine what needed to be done, I would let her know that I had truly heard her pain. I would only allow my problem-solver skills to shine through in the simple question, "What support do you need from me?"

I don't pride myself on fixing my friends' problems anymore. I'm happy to say that I'm so much better at just listening.

Someone in my life deals with a severe mental illness. In the past, I often tried to help him by showing him what was "wrong" with his thinking and actions. I didn't realize it at the time, but I was mostly lecturing him instead of listening and understanding his point of view. I thought I was being a good influence, but real, positive influence travels in both directions, with neither person needing to be the "right" one. Discovering wisdom works best as a collaboration.

A few years ago, I took some training in listening. I learned that it's more valuable to reflect back what people say, and to show understanding without judgment. I learned that if I showed understanding of the other person's feelings and thoughts, that alone would ease their burden. I learned that acceptance and understanding aren't necessarily the same things as approval and agreement. We needn't be afraid that we are compromising our own views or knowledge when we simply choose to understand another's. In fact, the openness of understanding can strengthen our own point of view.

Lately I've been applying my new listening skills in conversations with my mentally ill loved one. I allow myself to relate to difficult things he experiences and have even tried to be honest when I see a bit of myself in him, when I see the same passions, fears, and mistakes. By backing off, I've gained more of his trust. By not pretending to have all the answers for him, I've strengthened our bond. Now I only give him my opinion if he asks for it, and I'm honest enough to tell him when I don't have a clue how to answer his question. And you know, I've learned a whole lot from him, too.

MAY 8

Challenge

Ask someone "How are you, *really*?" and then listen without trying to fix things, without any goal other than being there and fully hearing them.

For Reflection

Do you feel a need to "fix" people's problems when they share them with you? If so, why do you think that is?

How do you feel about yourself (and about other people) when they try to fix your problems?

What would you do or say to comfort a friend if you weren't focused on offering solutions?

How Did It Go?

Was it hard to simply listen without offering solutions? Do you think you helped more by listening than you would have if you tried to fix the situation?

MAY 9

Challenge

Let someone teach you something instead of needing to be the one who has all the answers.

For Reflection

Do you take pride in having answers and enjoy showing off what you know?

How often do you stop or correct people when they're talking, and why?

What do think this conveys to them—and what might you convey if you gave them a chance to teach you instead?

How Did It Go?

What did you learn from this person? Did you learn anything about yourself through this experience?

MAY 10

Challenge

Whenever the phone rings today, take two deep breaths and smile before answering so you greet the person with mindfulness and joy.

For Reflection

What type of energy did you bring to your last few phone conversations?

Were you able to fully focus on the person calling you—and why or why not?

How did you feel during and after the conversation, and how do you think they felt?

How Did It Go?

Did your phone conversations feel any different than usual?

MAY 11

Challenge

Start a conversation with someone who is long-winded and often takes a while to get to the point, and smile and nod while they're speaking instead of rushing them.

For Reflection

Have you ever rushed someone through a story and then felt bad later?

What kinds of things do you usually think when someone takes a while to get to the point?

What's something you could think instead as a reminder to listen fully—for however long it takes?

How Did It Go?

What did the other person talk about? Did your mind wander while they were talking?

MAY 12

Challenge

Think of someone you plan to talk to today. List below any personal biases that might compromise your ability to listen fully, without forming judgments in your head. For each, identify why you think you formed this bias and something you can do or tell yourself to challenge it.

Brainstorm: *Your biases might pertain to religion, politics, ethnicity, or marital status. For example, you may believe it's wrong to take government assistance, solely because your father abused it and failed to provide for your family when you were young. Recognizing this, you'll be better able to listen to a friend who's collected unemployment for months.*

How Did It Go?

Did you identify a bias you'd never acknowledged before? Did this exercise help you listen more fully, and less judgmentally?

MAY 13

Challenge

Choose a talk on TED.com on a subject you assume won't interest you so you can practice listening fully and keeping an open mind. (Bonus! Write down everything you remember after the talk ends to see how well you listened and how much you retained.)

For Reflection

How does it affect your ability to listen when you assume a topic won't interest you?

Have you ever assumed this only to be pleasantly surprised?

What types of things do you do when you've checked out mentally, and how do you think other people feel when they can tell you're not interested in what they have to say?

How Did It Go?

Were you able to listen fully and keep an open mind? Did you appreciate this talk more than you thought you would?

MAY 14

Challenge

Call someone to ask about their day, and do nothing but listen. Shut off your TV, shut down your computer, put away your knitting or crossword puzzle. Just listen.

For Reflection

Are you more likely to multitask in conversations if the other person can't see what you're doing? How does this affect your ability to focus?

Can you tell when someone else is multitasking while you're talking to them on the phone? If so, how, and how do you feel about this?

How might it benefit both you and the other person to focus fully, without any distractions?

How Did It Go?

Who did you call, and what did that person share with you? How did this experience differ from other phone calls when you've multitasked while talking?

I like to talk. A lot. If you let me, I would probably talk your ear off all day. As a creative grasshopper, my mind runs a mile a minute, and has no shortage of ideas to explore. But I've learned that a conversation in which people are talking, but not listening, is not really a conversation. It's selfish, unsatisfying, and does absolutely nothing to build real connections.

As much as I like to talk, what I really want is to connect. I talk about what I do because I crave appreciation and admiration. I want to inspire someone. I talk about what's on my mind because I want to know that I'm not alone. I want to feel accepted and validated. I talk about what I know because I want to show that I have something to offer. For me, talking is asking for attention, praise, acceptance, and love. But I have learned that talking is not always the way to get these things, and it's not really giving.

I may think that I'm inspiring my friend by telling her about what I do, but in reality, she has worries and mental blocks that are keeping her from applying the insights she may gain from my lengthy monologue. I may think that by sharing my opinion about everything under the sun I'm showing I'm a worthy conversation partner, but really, people have their own opinions, and feeling like their opinions are heard is much more valuable to them than listening to mine.

The reality is that listening is much more vulnerable for me than sharing even my best-kept secrets. When I'm listening, giving the other person my full attention, holding space for them, I feel vulnerable because they have control over the conversation. All of a sudden, I'm left open and naked. My thoughts are free to race, and keeping them focused on the other person is tough, just like meditating. Talking a mile a minute is so much easier.

By not spouting out my ideas and beliefs, I'm letting the other person form their own opinion of me instead of trying to direct it. I am "just me," and I can't put on a mask through my words, opinions, and knowledge.

I have learned that I don't need to let my ideas and systems march forward to create a better impression. I now know that everyone else is just as broken as I am, and the cracks only have as much importance as you give them. I don't need to always share a story of my own in order to connect. My heart knows how to connect without my help. I don't need to give everyone the brilliant solution that saves the day. I've learned that I can be most helpful when I just give people the space they so desperately seek; then they are free to discover their own solutions and are much more open to seeing and implementing them.

Learning to listen is a lifelong journey, one that is definitely not easy for a talkaholic like me. But the joy that comes with the rewards makes up for the pain and effort. Achievements are, after all, only worth as much as the time put in. Talking about my achievements, opinions, conclusions, and lessons learned is a lot of fun. But listening for an hour, really connecting, fully being there, and watching the other person relax, unfurl, and bloom is priceless.

MAY 15

Challenge

Make it a goal not to interrupt anyone today so you can show through your actions that their words are important to you.

Tip: *Check in with yourself while you're listening to others to be sure you're not merely waiting to talk.*

For Reflection

How often do you wait to talk instead of fully listening?

Do you ever get impatient when listening, and why do you think that is?

How does it affect your ability to really hear others when you plan what you're going to say before they finish?

How Did It Go?

Were you able to listen without interrupting others? Did people seem more at ease talking to you as a result?

MAY 16

Challenge

Whenever someone shares their thoughts and feelings today, ask a couple follow-up questions to learn more.

For Reflection

Have you ever felt like you needed to cut a story short because you weren't sure the other person wanted to hear more?

If so, how did you feel about yourself when you considered that maybe you were boring the other person?

How do you feel when people ask follow-up questions after you share your thoughts and feelings? Grateful for the attention? Eager to continue? Happy that they care?

How Did It Go?

What kinds of follow-up questions did you ask? Did others seem to appreciate your interest?

MAY 17

Challenge

Choose something to look for in the people you encounter today to train yourself to pay more attention to others.

Brainstorm: *You could look for people wearing a particular color, people with a certain hairstyle, or people speaking with a specific accent.*

For Reflection

How much of your environment do you think you usually tune out because it's familiar?

How does it affect your ability to connect with others when you're disconnected from your surroundings, essentially operating on autopilot?

How might your life improve if you felt more present in your environment, more focused on others, and less focused on your own thoughts?

How Did It Go?

Did you focus more on the people around you as a result of this exercise?

MAY 18

Challenge

Whenever someone talks to you today, plant your feet firmly on the ground and put your hands in your lap so you won't distract with fidgety energy.

Tip: *Avoid caffeine if it makes you jittery and breathe deeply when others are talking to help you stay calm and focused.*

For Reflection

What types of fidgety things, if any, do you often do with your hands or feet?

Do you ever find yourself doing this when others are talking to you?

Would you feel distracted if someone else did this while you were talking?

How Did It Go?

Were you tempted to fidget? Did grounding yourself physically affect your ability to listen fully?

MAY 19

Challenge

Spend five minutes listening to the sound of your own breath to help calm your mind so you can better listen to others.

For Reflection

Have you ever had to repeat yourself because someone was there, but clearly lost in their own thoughts?

What did you feel as a result?

How does it benefit you when someone listens fully, and you suspect they're not thinking about anything else?

How Did It Go?

Did you feel more present and better able to listen after practicing deep breathing?

MAY 20

Challenge

Give someone a small gift that you know they'll like because they mentioned it in a previous conversation.

For Reflection

Who in your life could use a thoughtful gesture like this?

What's something they've shared with you that matters to them—something they may think you don't even remember?

Why is this so important to them?

How Did It Go?

What gift did you give, and how did the other person respond?

MAY 21

Challenge

Spend a little time clearing your mental clutter by writing down everything that's on your mind so that you can release your worries and be more present in conversations today.

What's on your mind?

How Did It Go?

Do you feel that your worries have less of a grip on you now that you've taken some time to purge them in this way?

One night while I was working as a waitress, a group of two men and two women came into the restaurant. One of the women pointed to a menu, and then at a booth. I nodded, smiling, and encouraged them to sit. I quickly discovered that they were speaking French, a language I barely knew.

Their faces were hidden behind their menus and my cheerful "Hi, how are you?" was met with silence. My confidence wavered slightly, but I decided to go out on a limb. In my poor French accent, I ventured, "Parlez-vous français?" Their seemingly cold demeanor vanished as all of their faces lit up. They looked at me with bright, eager eyes and said, "Oui!" With a relieved laugh, I said, "I understand a little!"

The rest of the evening was more fun than I could have imagined, as figuring out their food and drink orders turned into a game. When I guessed correctly, they all laughed appreciatively and cheered. And when I tried to use my limited French, they listened carefully and encouraged me.

We may have had a language barrier between us, but ironically enough, that's what broke down the wall that usually stands between strangers. The act of communicating with one another was a challenge that required attentiveness, listening, vulnerability, and most of all, acceptance of each other. The words didn't matter; we connected through our smiles, our laughs, and our open hearts. That night, we weren't strangers meeting for the first time; we were friends.

When the group was readying to leave, one of the women looked at me. I wanted her to know how happy I was that I'd met them. I gathered my courage and told her the only way I knew how. I said, "J'aime vous," which means, "I love you." She gave me a beautiful smile, gently squeezed my arm, and said, "Me too." The warm memory of that night reminds me to keep an open heart as I go through life. Love and understanding can be found anywhere, even when you least expect it.

We live in a society that values success. We create a thorough agenda packed with tasks that no one person can complete. It's understandable; biologically speaking, we are wired to contribute to our community because it lessens our likelihood of being left behind. There's no checklist for love, though, and this makes it one of the hardest areas of our life to confidently sink into. Brené Brown, author of *Daring Greatly,* speaks to this from the perspective of vulnerability. Subconsciously, we believe that we have to go beyond our means in order to be noticed. We strive to be extraordinary so that we have a reason to be loved instead of left behind.

I'm just as guilty of trying to prove myself to the world with my laundry list of to-do's that never feels complete. Ironically enough, spending time with my partner is something that rarely makes it onto the checklist. How is it possible that the person who fills my heart with love is someone I never fill my time with?

He brought it to my attention a few weeks ago when he told me that all of my attention was on my work. I told him that I was doing it for us, for our financial stability. After three days of arguing, I realized I was lying to him and to myself. Sure, the financial support is a bonus, but my work was in vain because I believed it made me more worthy of his love.

The truth is, he's grateful for the work but he loves me most when we are laughing, talking, and doing nothing of tangible importance. And there it is, simultaneously simple and so complex. You can't check off a list of tasks to ensure you are giving and receiving love. It's an intangible quality, a feeling, and it can't be measured.

MAY 22

Challenge

Whenever someone talks to you today, put down your phone or move away from your computer; or, if you can't talk at that moment, tell them when you'll be able to give them your full attention.

For Reflection

How often do you use technology during conversations with other people?

What might you conclude about yourself, the other person, and your relationship if someone regularly did this during conversations with you?

What might you conclude about yourself, the other person, and your relationship if they gave you their complete attention instead?

How Did It Go?

How did it affect your conversations to remove the distraction of technology?

MAY 23

Challenge

Ask someone about their day and then e-mail or call them later, recalling specific details from their story to show that you care.

For Reflection

Have you ever felt like someone wasn't really interested when they asked, "How was your day?"

What gave you this impression?

What could they have done differently to convey that they truly were interested?

How Did It Go?

What did the other person share, and which details did you recall later? Do you think they appreciated that you cared enough to do this?

MAY 24

Challenge

Write below one to three things that make it difficult to give people your full attention, and for each, one thing you can do to address that. Consciously choose to do these things today.

Brainstorm: *If you find it hard to pay attention because you cram too much into your schedule and frequently feel you should be doing something else, you could choose to say no to a request today. If you find it hard to pay attention because your mind wanders, you could set aside a few minutes for meditation to help you stay focused.*

1. I find it hard to pay attention because:

   I could address this by:

2. I find it hard to pay attention because:

   I could address this by:

3. I find it hard to pay attention because:

   I could address this by:

How Did It Go?

What did you do to improve your ability to pay attention to others, and did it help?

MAY 25

Challenge

Add quality time with a loved one—even if it's just a half hour over coffee—to your to-do list today.

For Reflection

Do you usually prioritize quality time with loved ones as highly as you prioritize other tasks?

What would you want your loved ones to know about how important they are to you?

What would you need to do differently (or not do) to show them this through your actions?

How Did It Go?

What specifically did you schedule into your day, and what was most enjoyable about it?

MAY 26

Challenge

Tell a friend, "I love that you . . ." and then finish the sentence with something not everyone may notice or appreciate about them.

For Reflection

Has anyone ever said this to you?

What did they point out, and how did you feel as a result?

What would the world be like if we all paid more attention to what we love about each other, and less attention to the things we don't like?

How Did It Go?

Who did you say this to, and how did you finish the sentence? How did they respond?

MAY 27

Challenge

Pay attention to your body and give it what it needs.

Brainstorm: *If you feel light-headed, you may need to drink a glass of water to hydrate; if your legs feel sore, you may need to get up and move around for a bit; if you feel exhausted, you may need to take a quick nap—even ten minutes in your car on a break can help!*

For Reflection

Do you regularly pay attention to what your body needs? If not, what prevents you from doing this?

How does it benefit you—physically, mentally, and emotionally—when you take care of your physical needs in this way?

What types of physical activities help you feel strong, balanced, and healthy?

How Did It Go?

What did you do for your body, and how did you feel as a result?

MAY 28

Challenge

Smile and nod at every street vendor or person you pass to let them know you see them.

For Reflection

How often are you so caught up in your head that you don't notice the people around you?

What thoughts or feelings often cause you to get wrapped up in yourself?

How might it benefit you and the people you encounter to let those thoughts and feelings go, and simply be, in the moment, with them?

How Did It Go?

What did you feel when smiling and nodding at others? Did anyone smile and nod back?

MAY 29

Challenge

Identify someone you haven't been giving your full attention to lately, and tell them, "I know I've been a little distracted in our conversations lately. Sorry about that. You deserve my full attention, and I intend to give it going forward."

For Reflection

What, if anything, has been distracting you and making it hard to focus?

What would you need to do for yourself to be able to focus better?

Why do your loved ones deserve your full attention?

How Did It Go?

What did the other person say after you apologized? Do you think you'll be more likely to focus now that you've acknowledged, out loud, that you haven't been giving this person your full attention?

MAY 30

Challenge

Whenever you talk to someone you know today, pretend you are meeting for the first time, and notice how that allows you to see them with fresh eyes.

For Reflection

How might you see your closest loved ones if you discarded all the judgments, opinions, and conclusions you've formed about them over the years?

What would you say or do differently if you were meeting them for the first time?

What might you notice or appreciate that you rarely do, now that you've known them so long?

How Did It Go?

Did you see anything in the people around you that you hadn't seen in a while?

MAY 31

Challenge

Pay attention to someone you usually disregard and then start a conversation with them about something you notice.

Brainstorm: *If you notice a neighbor seems frazzled, you could ask what's on their mind; if you notice your coworker has a picture of her family on her desk, you could ask about her children.*

For Reflection

What thoughts or behaviors prevent you from noticing and commenting on other people's lives?

How do you feel when other people notice and comment on what's going on in yours?

How might you affect someone's day for the better by showing through your actions that you see them and you care?

How Did It Go?

What did you notice, and what did you say? Was it gratifying to connect with this person on a meaningful level, and do you think it was gratifying for them?

MONTHLY REVIEW

- Which challenges were the most helpful for you, and why?
- Which challenges were the most difficult for you, and why?
- What did you learn about yourself through the process of completing these challenges? Did you form any new insights about listening and paying attention to people?
- What did you learn about the people in your life?
- Did these challenges strengthen your relationships, and how?
- Did you identify any areas for improvement and growth?
- Head over to http://tinybuddha.com/love-forums to share your experiences with other readers!

JUNE

Honesty and Trust

Reflections from LINDA CARVALHO

I used to be someone who avoided conflict with others at all costs. I was passive by nature, and I shied away from standing up for my beliefs and voicing my opinions. I longed for the ability to express myself freely. And I deeply admired and looked up to my sister, who possessed the internal strength to be truthful, regardless of the consequences.

Sometimes my sister wasn't sure if she was pushing others away because of her honest and strong-minded nature. She'd often find herself in situations where she would lose friends. Perhaps her opinions were too much to handle. When she would come to me in full-blown tears, asking me, "Why do my friends keep leaving? Why don't they understand that I'm just trying to help them?" I would respond to her by saying, "They don't want to hear the truth from you, because sometimes the truth hurts."

I know now that my opinions matter and have the right to be heard. But I also realize it's not just what you say to others that matters; it's also the manner in which you say it, because it's not always easy to accept the truth. I have learned that choosing your words carefully and being mindful of your tone is the key to flourishing relationships.

When I engage in conversations, I always try my best to think before I speak. Then, I contemplate, *Is it worth saying? How will what I say make a difference to this person?* If I proceed to give my opinion, I then decide, *How can I say this in such as way that it comes across as genuine, yet constructive?* Speaking up for what we believe and sharing our opinions can be helpful and beneficial—when it's appropriate, kind, and constructive.

A while back, my husband walked into the kitchen where I was reading an article on my phone and asked me if I had a chance to get a Father's Day card for his dad. I said I didn't, and, since it was eight in the evening, I'd get it tomorrow. He put on his shoes, got the keys, and said, "I'm just going to get it," then slammed the door. Immediately, my mind started racing about how I had messed up. How I place more emphasis on my own family, and he must feel I don't do enough for his. I was spiraling into negativity and, within minutes, I was in a dark place of believing I'm not good enough.

That night, I asked my husband if he was upset. He responded no, but that he had felt the need to go get the card that instant. I brought up slamming the door, and that it made me feel like there was more to the story. He agreed that he was upset because I didn't look up from my phone to answer the question. AHHH, relief! He just wanted my full attention during a conversation. He doesn't think I'm the daughter-in-law or wife from hell. I asked why he didn't just ask me, and he said he felt like I should've known.

There were so many miscommunications like this between us. And I'd get upset and then let it go, without stating what I really thought or felt. I realized I needed more openness in our conversations. More direct communication about what we really mean to say rather than expecting that I "should just know." If he tells me exactly what he needs from me, and I from him, there is no interference, no misinformation, and no blame, shame, or guilt in either one of us.

This simple interaction of talking openly and honestly completely transformed our marriage. The energy around us has become light, and we are able to accept the love that is between us.

JUNE 1

Challenge

Share an opinion or piece of feedback, choosing words that are kind, constructive, and helpful.

For Reflection

If you've hesitated to share your opinions in the past, what has held you back?

Can you think of some times when you shared your opinion and later felt glad you did? Why did you feel this way?

Who do you know who freely and tactfully shares their opinions, and what do you admire about how they do this?

How Did It Go?

What opinion did you share, and how did the other person respond? Did you learn anything through this experience that will help you share your opinion more openly going forward?

JUNE 2

Challenge

Be honest with someone about something you need in a relationship. Express this in a way that does not imply the other person is currently doing something wrong.

Brainstorm: *This might be something physical, like help with household chores, or something intangible, like clearer communication.*

For Reflection

In which relationship have you hesitated to clearly communicate your needs, and why?

Would you want to know other people's needs so you could try to meet them?

How might your relationships improve if you were honest about your needs—and how might your life improve if you were honest *with yourself* when, deep down, you knew someone's actions proved that your needs simply weren't important to them?

How Did It Go?

What need did you share, and did the other person seem open to meeting it? Do you feel differently about this relationship after communicating what you need?

JUNE 3

Challenge

Make today an excuse-free day and be honest with people about why you want or don't want to do something. (Be sure to also avoid making excuses to yourself!)

For Reflection

What excuses have you recently used to avoid doing things you didn't want to do?

Why did you use these excuses instead of telling people the truth?

How do excuses cause more hassle than they save and put wedges in relationships?

How Did It Go?

How did it feel to be honest instead of making excuses? Did others seem to appreciate your honesty?

JUNE 4

Challenge

Identify a lie you recently told a loved one, and why you told that lie. Now share this with that person so that you'll get closer to addressing the underlying issue.

Brainstorm: *If you told your significant other that you weren't angry when you were, acknowledging how you really feel could lead to him changing his hurtful behavior; if you told a friend you were busy because she asks for your help a lot, admitting this could help create a more balanced relationship.*

For Reflection

What did you hope to gain in telling this lie?

What pain did you hope to avoid?

How could holding on to this lie actually cause more pain, for you or the other person?

How Did It Go?

Were you able to address the underlying issue? If so, does your relationship feel stronger?

JUNE 5

Challenge

Write below all the ways you've lied in the past to make yourself look better, why you think you've lied about these things, and how this has negatively affected you and your relationships. Remember these things as you go about your day as a reminder to be truthful instead of trying to manipulate perception.

Brainstorm: *You may have exaggerated your accomplishments, downplayed your flaws or mistakes, or pretended to know more than you do.*

How Did It Go?

Did you form any new insights about yourself that will help you be more truthful going forward?

JUNE 6

Challenge

Be honest about something you usually wouldn't admit.

Brainstorm: *For example, if you drift off when someone's talking, say, "I spaced out. Can you start again?" If someone invites you out but you want to veg and watch reality TV, say, "I actually want to sit on my couch and watch reruns of* The Real Housewives *all night."*

For Reflection

What types of things are you hesitant to admit, and why?

What do you fear these things say about you as a person?

Why might others appreciate your honesty about these things?

How Did It Go?

What were you honest about, and how did the other person respond? Did this feel liberating?

JUNE 7

Challenge

Be honest with yourself about how you feel right now and embrace the feeling, without trying to make it go away. After a short while, reflect on what this feeling is trying to teach you, and if possible, act on what you've learned.

Tip: *Try to peel back the layers of your emotions. There may be loneliness underneath anger, or there may be a feeling of inadequacy underneath jealousy.*

For Reflection

Do you find it difficult to identify what you're really feeling? If so, why do you think that is?

Do you allow yourself to fully feel your emotions, or do you usually try to make them go away as quickly as possible? If you chose the latter, why do you think you do this, and how does this negatively affect you?

How Did It Go?

What feeling did you discover? What did you learn from this, and how did you act on that knowledge?

When I first moved in with my best friend, anger terrified me. I thought that raised voices automatically meant a relationship was on the rocks, and I would often run away before the other person could (or so I anticipated) drop me first. My friend, on the other hand, defaulted to anger. This scared me away, and then she would get frustrated when I refused to engage with her.

When I finally worked up the courage to express how I felt, my friend had a hard time taking what I said at face value. In her family, "It's all right" would usually be accompanied by a heavy sigh and body language that screamed how *not* all right it was. Unused to people who simply spoke their minds with no ulterior motive, my friend often attributed intentions to me that weren't true. This felt like she was calling me a liar, and I resented that deeply.

What saved us during those first years, and what continues to provide the foundation of our friendship almost a decade later, is a combination of honesty and trust. We've committed to always be up front with each other about what we're feeling, trust that the other person is being truthful, and keep talking things out until any issues are resolved.

I've learned to trust the fact that she won't abandon me or strike out in hurtful ways even when she's upset with me. And she has learned to believe that we can both say what we mean, with faith that the other person will take it seriously and be willing to talk it out like adults rather than play the martyr or toss around implications of guilt.

If you'd like to firm up the foundations of one of your own close relationships, don't be afraid to be the one to reach out first. Let the other person know that you trust them enough to always be honest with them, and assure them that they can feel comfortable doing the same with you. It's hard to react negatively to that kind of forthrightness, and you'll give them the chance to respond in kind.

When I was a child, I was part of a family that didn't communicate beyond "pass the salt." There was no confiding of fears, sharing of hopes, and encouraging each other's dreams. Now, as an adult, I find it can be really hard not to provide stock answers to my husband's questions. I am "fine," all is "okay," I have "everything" I need. To realize that I can contribute to a conversation—that I am valued, and somebody actually wants to delve inside my head (which can be a scary place), and yet love me and want to know more—is an exhilarating and sometimes terrifying experience.

I have spent such a large portion of my life feeling like I am not worth listening to, and I have always considered myself a private person, used to keeping my thoughts and feelings inside. But there is a huge difference between privacy and secrecy.

I acquired a disability after an accident, and it is something I tried to keep hidden for a long time. I felt ashamed because my body no longer functioned in the way I thought it should. It would have been okay had I not wanted to talk about my disability for privacy's sake. But secrecy is something very different entirely. Keeping a secret is about fearfully hiding something from the world, separating yourself, and that takes a lot of energy.

Slowly I learned to be more open and honest and to explore my feelings, and now I feel such a sense of peace and acceptance. I realize the human body is just a place we inhabit in this lifetime. It doesn't actually define who I am.

It is perfectly okay to be private, of course; you don't need to share any more than you feel comfortable. To lay yourself open takes courage, but when there is nothing left to keep hidden, nothing to fear, it can be one of the most liberating things you can do for yourself.

JUNE 8

Challenge

Share a secret with someone you believe to be trustworthy, even something small, to help establish mutual trust.

For Reflection

How has keeping this secret caused you pain?

What have you feared you might lose if you shared this secret?

What do you stand to gain if you let someone in?

How Did It Go?

What secret did you share, and how did it feel to let someone in?

JUNE 9

Challenge

Make it a goal not to tell a single white lie to anyone today.

For Reflection

For what reasons have you told white lies in the past?

Has a white lie ever put a wedge in one of your relationships? How?

Would you trust someone if you knew they told *you* white lies?

How Did It Go?

Were you tempted to tell any white lies? Did anything positive come from being 100 percent truthful?

JUNE 10

Challenge

Think about a recent time when you were passive-aggressive instead of honestly communicating what frustrated or annoyed you. Write below what happened and any fears or beliefs that may have prevented you from being clear and direct. Then write how being passive-aggressive affected your relationship and prevented you from resolving the issue. Keep these things in mind today as a reminder to avoid passive-aggressive behavior and clearly communicate your thoughts instead.

How Did It Go?

Did you form any helpful new insights as a result of completing this exercise? Were you tempted to be passive-aggressive at any point today? What happened as a result of communicating more clearly?

JUNE 11

Challenge

Thank someone in your life for being honest with you about something, especially if you imagine it was hard for them, to encourage future honesty.

For Reflection

Why do you appreciate when people are honest with you?

Why may it have been difficult for this person to share this specific thing with you?

How did their honesty help you or enable you to help them?

How Did It Go?

How did the other person respond when you expressed your gratitude?

JUNE 12

Challenge

Share your true motivations for something you recently said or did (or didn't say or do) that was hurtful.

Brainstorm: *For example, you may have snapped at someone because their action triggered something painful from your past, or you may have skipped a friend's celebratory dinner because you were jealous.*

For Reflection

Can you think of a time when someone was honest with you in this way?

If so, did you appreciate this honesty, and why?

What would you need to believe about yourself or your loved ones to embrace this kind of self-awareness and honesty?

How Did It Go?

What did you acknowledge, and how did the other person respond? Do you feel it strengthened your relationship to nurture this kind of self-awareness and share it?

JUNE 13

Challenge

Be honest with yourself about what you most want to change in your life and why you haven't done this yet. Then identify one thing you can do to work toward this today, and do it.

For Reflection

How have you been trying to protect yourself by lying to yourself?

How has lying to yourself in this way actually hurt you?

What would your ninety-year-old self tell your current self about making a change, starting now?

How Did It Go?

What did you learn about yourself, and what did you do to begin creating change?

JUNE 14

Challenge

Be honest about something you don't know.

Brainstorm: *If a coworker or client asks a question and you don't know the answer, admit this and tell them you'll figure it out and get back to them; if a friend brings up a topic that's unfamiliar to you, acknowledge you don't know much about it instead of pretending you do just to look good.*

For Reflection

Are you usually honest with others when you don't know something? If not, why?

How might it benefit you to acknowledge when you don't know something?

Why might others appreciate this honesty?

How Did It Go?

What did you admit not knowing? How did it feel to do this, and how did the other person respond?

I work as an intern-counselor at a residential high school with around seventy teenagers. Many of them have come from unbelievably challenging backgrounds where they have had to learn to not trust anyone as a matter of survival. Imagine having spent your entire life always having to watch your back literally and figuratively, not just because there are strangers who may want to harm you, but also because even those who are supposed to be close to you could turn against you in an instant. How difficult do you think it would be to let down the defenses that kept you safe, and in some cases alive, for so long?

I've struggled with allowing people to really know me because for most of my life, it felt as though I was burned every time I did. Over time, I learned how to seem friendly but kept virtually everyone at a distance, and those who got too close I rapidly pushed away, sometimes completely out of my life.

I was already struggling to put my pieces back together after several major tragedies in my family, and allowing others in meant the possibility of compounding my heartbreak. I just couldn't handle any more at the time. Eventually, I began to open up, but each time found myself wondering why I had been so naive.

Then there came a point where, slowly but surely, people began to enter my life who showed me what it meant to be able to trust. They showed me I could trust them to show up, trust them to listen, trust them with commitments, and the biggest one of all, trust them with my heart.

If I wouldn't have started removing my walls, I may have never found these amazing people. They didn't appear because I had perfectly learned to trust already. They appeared because I was willing to learn to trust, even if imperfectly.

As I've been learning to trust and lower my defenses, I've been working with my students to do the same. Their stories are different in that many of them have come from a history of abuse and/or gang-related activities. But we share a similar outcome in struggling to realize that what once protected us is no longer needed, and in some cases, is actually hurting us more by isolating us from the love we need to heal and move forward.

We each come to crossroads in our lives where we have to make the decision to let go of our old survival mechanisms in order to grow and make room for something better. Sometimes what used to protect us becomes what harms us and stifles the capacity for our lives to be open and full of joy, love, and peace.

When it comes to trusting each other, we have to accept that our past is not our present. We have to be able to recognize that what hurt us before is not necessarily what is currently standing before us—even sometimes when the situation looks frighteningly similar, and sometimes even when it's the same person.

Does this mean we won't ever get hurt again? Nope. That's a part of life. People will let us down, and we will let them down, but that doesn't mean our efforts to disassemble our defense mechanisms are in vain. If we never allow ourselves any vulnerability, we lose out on the opportunity to make incredibly deep and meaningful connections that open up our lives in ways that couldn't happen any other way.

Those connections draw out the very best within and create a new reality—one where we learn that the only way to know if you can trust somebody is to trust them.

JUNE 15

Challenge

Ask a friend or loved one to do something important for you to show them you trust them.

For Reflection

Do you easily trust others to do important things for you, or are you more apt to try to do it all yourself?

How does it negatively affect you when you try to do too much on your own?

How might it benefit your relationships to entrust people in this way?

How Did It Go?

Was it hard to entrust someone with something important? Are you glad you did, and if so, why?

JUNE 16

Challenge

Observe those around you today, and watch for signs that people are good—little words or acts of kindness that show you people are looking out for you and others.

For Reflection

Do you believe that people are basically good?

How does your belief about people affect the way you experience the world?

How might it make a difference in your day, and how might it affect the people around you, if you look for signs that people care?

How Did It Go?

What did you observe? Are these things you might not have noticed if you weren't consciously looking for them?

JUNE 17

Challenge

Spend a few minutes in reflection, and identify one way you've been betrayed in a past relationship that's led you to mistrust people. Now write down an affirmation to break this pattern and read it several times throughout the day.

Brainstorm: *For example, "I choose not to make other people pay for ________________'s mistakes."*

For Reflection

Do you believe this past betrayal reflects a truth about people in general or the world at large?

How does this belief negatively affect you and your current relationships?

What might your life be like if you no longer believed this was true?

How Did It Go?

Did reading this affirmation throughout the day affect your state of mind and how you engaged with others?

JUNE 18

Challenge

Identify a person you've kept in your life who has betrayed you. Now give them a small opportunity to regain your trust, knowing there are no guarantees, and trusting that you can handle whatever happens.

Brainstorm: *You could share your feelings with this person, invite them to something that means a lot to you, or ask for help with something important.*

For Reflection

Why are you maintaining this relationship, in spite of what happened?

Does it benefit either of you to hold on to this relationship *and* the past?

What would need to happen for you to trust this person again?

How Did It Go?

What did you entrust this person with, and how did they handle it? Did this experience help you rebuild trust, even if just a little?

JUNE 19

Challenge

Give everyone the benefit of the doubt today instead of assuming they have poor intentions.

For Reflection

Can you think of a time when you assumed someone had poor intentions but later learned you were wrong?

How did this affect your relationship?

What did you learn from this experience that can help you give people the benefit of the doubt going forward?

How Did It Go?

Were you tempted to think the worst of someone today? If so, why, and were you able to challenge your assumptions?

JUNE 20

Challenge

Instead of discussing a frustration or annoyance behind someone's back, go directly to the source to get it resolved.

For Reflection

How would you feel if you learned that someone was upset with you and talked to others behind your back? Would you wish that person had spoken to you instead?

What does it accomplish to complain about someone to others who aren't involved?

What might it accomplish if you share your feelings with this person instead?

How Did It Go?

Were you tempted to complain about someone behind their back? If so, were you able to confront them instead? If not, what prevented you from doing this, and how can you work on this going forward?

JUNE 21

Challenge

Keep a promise to yourself today.

Brainstorm: *For example, exercise, because you planned to, don't call the person you told yourself you wouldn't call, or look for a new job instead of making excuses to push it off.*

For Reflection

Is this a promise you've struggled to keep, and if so, why?

What would you need to do (or not do) to prioritize this today?

How do you feel about yourself when you don't keep your promises to yourself, and when you do?

How Did It Go?

What promise to yourself did you keep, and how did you feel about yourself as a result?

When I was a young man, I felt anxious about how much any girlfriend cared for me, which, in turn, became outright jealousy and resulted in controlling behavior. I worried that my girlfriend was going to leave me for another man, and then I became aggressive. I acted out when she wanted to go out with her friends. If we went out together, I would fly into a rage when we got home if she had so much as glanced at other men.

All this behavior was about demanding, without explicitly saying it, that she demonstrate how much she loved me. I acted this way because, despite all the evidence to the contrary, I believed she did not. I decided I was the victim and became moody, sulky, withdrawn, and passive-aggressive, yet again manipulating my environment to get the attention I craved. Negative attention was better than nothing. Yet if I lost all attention because of my behavior, I was okay with that. I would have preferred to be alone and know I was right than be in a relationship and live with the fear that I was not good enough. But once I was alone again, I wanted a relationship to prove that I was lovable.

I tried to control the fear that I was unlovable by controlling the person I loved. I even took to confronting men who I saw as a threat. By threatening and controlling other men, I could control my girlfriend and thus control my own fear. It seemed logical at the time. As you may have guessed, it had the opposite effect. My attempts to control the women I dated ended up driving them away. Either they would end the relationship or I would before they did. Sometimes my behavior drove them toward other men. I made them feel so unsafe that the only safe way to leave me was to have some protection in the form of someone else.

Then one day, after a lengthy period of learning and reflecting on the repetitive patterns in my relationships, I realized that I could not control my girlfriends, since control is an illusion, and that trying to control them had the opposite effect. I understood that I can't make someone love me by fearing they won't, and fearing someone may be unfaithful will not ensure that they won't be. I also recognized that my fear was often greater than the things I worried about. Lastly, I realized that I needed to learn to love myself and stop expecting others to do something I wasn't doing for myself.

As a result of some intense personal development work, I started to acknowledge and appreciate my strengths and validate myself in the way I'd hoped others would; in turn, my fear subsided and has all but left. Now I choose to trust my girlfriend. I have no more control over her than if I chose to be suspicious, needy, and fearful. By choosing to trust her I remove the fear, let go of control, and can enjoy the relationship for what it is. We can choose to live in fear or not—that's something we can control. And we can also control if we choose to be miserable or happy. I choose happy.

JUNE 22

Challenge

Write below everything you'd need to believe about yourself to trust that people truly love you and wouldn't intentionally hurt you. Then identify one positive thing you can do for yourself to reinforce these beliefs—and do it today.

Brainstorm: *For example, if you write that you're worthy of love, you could reinforce this by asking someone for a hug; if you write below that you're good enough just as you are, you could reinforce this by trying something you've always wanted to try but haven't because you feared you weren't good enough.*

How Did It Go?

What did you choose to do to reinforce these beliefs? Did this exercise affect your feelings about yourself or your relationships in a positive way?

JUNE 23

Challenge

Do something helpful for someone else without wanting or expecting anything in return, and vocalize this to them to show they can trust you to be there for them, without ulterior motives.

Brainstorm: *Teach someone to do something you know they want to learn, offer to help them declutter or clean their house, or volunteer to help a coworker with a difficult task.*

For Reflection

When was the last time someone did something for you without wanting or expecting anything in return?

Did you trust that they didn't have ulterior motives? Why or why not?

How did this selfless act affect your feelings for them?

How Did It Go?

How did the other person respond to your selfless offer?

JUNE 24

Challenge

Leave a comment on a blog post, forum post, or social media update where the writer shared their struggles and insights, sharing how their honesty was helpful to you.

For Reflection

What do you think is the most difficult part about sharing one's struggles in a public forum?

What do you find admirable or inspiring about this?

How does it help when someone is honest enough to admit their struggles and what they've learned from them?

How Did It Go?

What did you write in your comment? Did the writer reply? If so, was this exchange helpful?

JUNE 25

Challenge

Make "Let go of control" your mantra today and repeat this in your head whenever you're tempted to nag or micromanage someone.

For Reflection

Can you think of a recent time when someone nagged or micromanaged you? How did you feel as a result, and how did this affect your relationship?

Is it hard for you to let go of control in this way? Why do you think that is, and how can you work on that?

How might the people around you benefit if you adopted this mantra and acted on it?

How Did It Go?

Were you able to let go a little more than usual? What, if anything, made this hard for you?

JUNE 26

Challenge

In conversations with others, practice hearing their thoughts and feelings without getting defensive or oversensitive, to teach them it's safe to be honest with you.

For Reflection

Can you think of a time when someone got defensive with you when you were sharing your honest thoughts and feelings?

How did you feel about sharing the truth with them, knowing they'd get defensive?

Would you rather people be honest with you, or that they say what you want to hear?

How Did It Go?

Were you tempted to get defensive today? Were you able to challenge this instinct, and if so, how did this affect your conversations?

JUNE 27

Challenge

Answer all calls, e-mails, and texts today—even if not right away—to show people that they can trust you to be there for them. If you can't be there for them because you're focusing your energy on your own needs, share this information with them.

For Reflection

For what reasons have you ignored calls or texts in the past?

Do you feel comfortable letting people know when you're focusing on your own needs, or you don't feel mentally or emotionally capable of being there for them?

How does it affect your relationships when you don't share these things with them, and how might your relationships improve if you did?

How Did It Go?

Who called, e-mailed, or texted, and how were you there for them?

JUNE 28

Challenge

Identify someone you've blamed for something recently, at work or in your personal life. Now be honest with yourself about what you could have done differently, even if it's something small, and share this with that person.

For Reflection

Do you believe there's always a right person and a wrong person, or that there's often room for improvement on both ends?

When you've blamed others in the past, without taking responsibility for anything you could have done differently, how have they responded?

How do you feel when someone takes responsibility for their part instead of placing all the blame on you?

How Did It Go?

What did you take responsibility for, and did this help resolve the issue?

JUNE 29

Challenge

Lend something to someone to show you trust them with your things.

Brainstorm: *You could lend a book, a piece of clothing, your camera, or even your car.*

For Reflection

Do you feel comfortable lending people your things? Why or why not?

When was the last time someone lent something to you? What did you most appreciate about this?

What would you need to believe or let go to feel comfortable lending something of yours to someone else?

How Did It Go?

What did you lend, and to whom? Did they seem to appreciate that you trusted them with this?

JUNE 30

Challenge

Commit to doing something for someone in the future so that when you follow through, they will know they can trust you to do what you say you'll do.

Brainstorm: *Offer to babysit someone's kids, drive a friend to an appointment, or help them move or paint a room.*

For Reflection

Have you ever been in a relationship or friendship with someone who rarely committed to anything? If so, how did you feel about that relationship?

What does it say about a relationship when someone is willing to make commitments and follow through?

Do you regularly commit to do things in the future, or do you avoid commitments? If you chose the latter, why do you think that is?

How Did It Go?

What did you commit to do? Did the other person accept your offer, and did they seem to appreciate it?

MONTHLY REVIEW

- Which challenges were the most helpful for you, and why?
- Which challenges were the most difficult for you, and why?
- What did you learn about yourself through the process of completing these challenges? Did you form any new insights about being honest and trustworthy?
- What did you learn about the people in your life?
- Did these challenges strengthen your relationships, and how?
- Did you identify any areas for improvement and growth?
- Head over to http://tinybuddha.com/love-forums to share your experiences with other readers!

JULY

Kindness and Thoughtfulness

Reflections from LORI DESCHENE

It's rare to know a person who embodies every quality you aspire to possess, but I was privileged to know such a woman for over thirty years. My grandmother was extraordinary in her capacity to appreciate the ordinary, and she was always fully *there*—present, smiling, and available to others, no matter where she was.

She touched everyone in our family, and not just because she was the eternally nurturing matriarch who always greeted us with smiling eyes and a hug. It was because she treated *everyone* with that same warmth and kindness, seeing the best in all and giving to all the best she had to give. She listened fully, accepted wholly, and never seemed to judge. And she gave indiscriminately, conveying through her generosity that everyone was worthy of her love.

I'd like to think that I carry within me a piece of my grandmother's kindhearted spirit. If so, I'm far from alone, as I see it reflecting back to me from all corners of my family. And my grandmother surely saw it, as well, before she left us at eighty-two.

One specific occasion comes to mind, though I wasn't there to witness it. My mother, aunt, and cousin were driving my grandmother back to the rehab facility where she was recovering from a broken hip. Grammy asked if they could stop at a popular coffee chain to buy donuts and muffins for the nurses. She appreciated them, both for doing their jobs and for treating her with care. And true to form, she sought to return that kindness with a small gesture of appreciation.

My cousin Katie said she would run into the store to get the things Grammy requested. Grammy handed her a reloadable gift card and told Katie she'd give her cash if the balance wasn't enough.

As my grandmother, mother, and aunt sat in the car, they watched Katie through the window and saw her pull out her wallet.

"Must not have been enough on the card," Grammy said.

When Katie got back in the car, Grammy reached for her purse, ready to pay Katie back whatever she'd spent.

"Dear, I saw you give her some money," she said. "There wasn't enough on the card? What do I owe you?"

Katie said, "Oh, no. I didn't even ask about the card balance. I just gave her cash for the donuts and put another $20 on the card for you."

It was exactly the kind of thing Grammy would have done—and the kind of thing people often felt compelled to do for her. Thoughtfulness has a way of volleying from one heart to another and back.

There's a video online about acts of kindness that shows how one act leads to another and another—a construction worker helps a boy who fell off his skateboard, then the boy helps an older woman carry groceries across the street, then the woman gives change to a woman rifling through her purse at a meter, and so on.

Kindness is, quite literally, contagious. It inspires us to focus less on everything we think is bad about the world and more on what we can do to contribute to the good. And when we contribute to the good, we *feel* good—about our actions, about the joy we've given others, and about ourselves. And then we inspire others to create these good feelings for themselves and others. It creates a ripple effect that, much like the impact of one woman's life, can't possibly be measured. But it ripples on, powerfully, nonetheless.

JULY 1

Challenge

Buy a $5 gift card and carry it in your purse or wallet to give to someone you think would appreciate it. (If you don't have $5 to spare, look for a coupon online that you can e-mail or print to give to someone who may appreciate it.)

For Reflection

Has anyone ever given you a small gift for no reason?

If so, what did you appreciate about this?

If someone were to give you an unexpected gift card, what would you find most useful? Which business or type of product would it be?

How Did It Go?

What kind of gift card did you buy, and whom did you give it to? Do you think this brightened their day?

JULY 2

Challenge

Write down three simple pleasures that make you smile, and then incorporate them into your day.

Brainstorm: *For example, taking a bubble bath, walking barefoot on the beach, eating one of your favorite childhood snacks, or reading a book in the park.*

1.

2.

3.

How Did It Go?

Which simple pleasure did you most appreciate and enjoy, and why?

JULY 3

Challenge

Contact a loved one who experienced a tremendous loss in the last year to ask how they're doing. (Even months later, when others may assume they've healed, the pain can still feel overwhelming.)

For Reflection

How did this loss affect your loved one?

When was the last time you called them just to check in with them?

If it has been a while, is there a reason, such as you're afraid of dredging up their sadness, or you find the conversation uncomfortable? What can you tell yourself to help overcome this?

How Did It Go?

What did your loved one share with you? Did they seem to appreciate that you took the time to do this?

JULY 4

Challenge

Do something thoughtful for the kindest person you know.

Brainstorm: *Send a text just to say hi, bring this person a coffee, or write and mail a handwritten letter that expresses how much you value them.*

For Reflection

How does this person go above and beyond to be kind to others?

How has he or she made a difference in your life and the lives of other people?

What kind gesture would this person most appreciate from you, and why?

How Did It Go?

What thoughtful gesture did you choose, and how did the other person respond?

JULY 5

Challenge

Call or e-mail your oldest friend, just to let them know you are thinking of them.

For Reflection

When was the last time you spoke to your oldest friend?

What's the first thing that comes to mind when you think of them?

Why do you appreciate that this friendship has endured all these years?

How Did It Go?

Was your friend excited to hear from you? What did you talk about?

JULY 6

Challenge

Share with your significant other (or a loved one) author Gary Chapman's love languages, from the book *The Five Love Languages*. These are five different ways a person might like to receive love, including: words of affirmation, acts of service, receiving gifts, quality time, and physical touch. Then ask which one they most appreciate, and do something to give them this kind of love today.

Brainstorm: *If your loved one most appreciates words of affirmation, you could express your gratitude for the difference that person has made in your life; if your loved one most appreciates quality time, you could plan to take a walk together after work.*

For Reflection

What's your love language?

Why do you feel most loved when someone does this for you?

How might it improve your relationships if you knew all your loved ones' love languages—and frequently "spoke them"?

How Did It Go?

Were you surprised to learn your loved one's "love language"? How did you act on this today?

JULY 7

Challenge

Invite a loved one to join you in an act of kindness.

Brainstorm: *This could be something big, like running a marathon for a cause, or something smaller, like doing something thoughtful for a mutual friend.*

For Reflection

What's something you've considered doing to help or support someone you know, or a cause that's meaningful to you?

How do you believe you could make a difference by doing this?

Who in your life might be interested in joining you, and why?

How Did It Go?

Was this something you planned to do in the future, or something you did today? If the latter, how did it improve the experience to share it with someone else?

As I walked down a trendy suburban street heading to an appointment, my phone rang. I was not having the best of days. I was walking past chic cafés and designer shops displaying tempting wares; however, having been laid off for the second time in two years, with a mortgage to pay and months without an income, these trivial symbols of indulgence were almost too much to bear.

Answering the call, I realized that it was a promotional call from a reputed global charitable organization that I had supported over the last few years while I was employed. I expected it to be a request for donations. It irritated me that this man would call me and ask for money when I was counting every cent to make ends meet in one of the most expensive cities in the world. On a deeper level, my feelings of inadequacy were reinforced because I would have to deny his request. My mood began to darken.

As the young man with an attractive Irish accent chatted about an initiative to supply drinking water to millions around the world, I was tempted to hang up the phone. I was nearly at my appointment and I would not be able to chat for long anyway. How did it matter if I hung up? I was about to pull the phone away from my ear and hit the red button. But then something made me pause.

I reminded myself that the world does not revolve around me. The caller did not know my circumstances. He was simply doing his job. If I was rude to him, I was spreading ill will and negativity. He didn't deserve that. This was my chance, albeit a small one, to make a better decision. So I stayed on the line and listened to what he was saying. At the first opportunity, I let him know that I only had a few minutes free and I would have to end the call soon. He may have thought I was just making excuses, but he gamely continued on at a faster pace, which was somehow very endearing.

As I approached my destination, I apologized and excused myself from the conversation. My caller thanked me for my time and promised to call back some other time when I was not occupied. This small incident barely took up five minutes, but it significantly changed the direction of my day. I was happier for being respectful and polite to a stranger for a couple of minutes. Had I chosen to end the call abruptly, I would have carried that negativity for the rest of the day. Instead, an eager Irish chap brightened my day a little with his enthusiasm.

I have realized recently that every small thought, every decision, every step we take has a huge impact on us, and the world around us. The old me, with my sense of superiority and entitlement, would have hung up the phone without a second thought. The old me would have considered my time too worthwhile to waste on such a phone call, however good the cause. I have also realized that every interaction is an opportunity to do good and receive good. I urge you to make the effort to make every interaction a positive one, and to face the world with a smile and a kind word. If you throw kindness out into the world, it will bounce right back, only multiplied several times over.

JULY 8

Challenge

Be kind to a telemarketer who calls you today, or anyone who tries to sell you something or asks for a donation, even if you don't listen for long.

For Reflection

Have you ever responded rudely to a telemarketer or salesperson before?

What do you imagine it's like to work in this field?

What would you appreciate hearing if you were in their shoes and had already connected with many people who seemed annoyed?

How Did It Go?

Did you see telemarketers and salespeople differently today? How did this show in your words and actions?

JULY 9

Challenge

Write a positive review on Yelp for a business you frequent and enjoy.

For Reflection

How have the employees at this business gone above and beyond to create a positive experience?

What sets this business apart from others, and what could you highlight in your review to help them get new customers?

How might it benefit the whole community to support good people doing good things?

How Did It Go?

How do you feel you helped this business with your positive review?

JULY 10

Challenge

Be patient and understanding with people who serve you, especially if they have a lot of customers to tend to.

For Reflection

How do you usually respond when you receive slow service?

What might you think or feel if you were overwhelmed in your job, and you knew people were waiting on you?

What would you want to hear if you were in this position?

How Did It Go?

How do you think your patience made a difference for the people who served you? Did this exercise help you see them as not just people serving you, but fellow human beings doing their best?

JULY 11

Challenge

Smile and nod at another driver at a red light or, if you don't drive, give up your seat to someone on the train or bus.

For Reflection

How do you feel at the start of a long commute or after a long day?

Can you think of a time when someone seemed especially friendly on the road or on public transportation? How did it improve your day or affect you for the better?

What keeps you from treating other commuters with kindness and compassion?

How Did It Go?

How did you feel when doing this, and how did the other person respond? Do you think you made their commute a little less stressful?

JULY 12

Challenge

End every (nonwork-related) phone conversation today with "I love you," "I'll be thinking of you," or "I always enjoy talking to you!"

For Reflection

How often do you say these things to people you care about?

How does it make you feel when someone says one of these things to you?

What might the world be like if everyone felt these things?

How Did It Go?

Did you feel closer to others as a result of ending calls this way? How did other people respond?

JULY 13

Challenge

Schedule a window of technology-free time into your day, as an act of kindness to yourself. Plan an activity that nourishes you physically, mentally, emotionally, or spiritually.

Brainstorm: *Stretching may nourish you physically; sitting in nature breathing deeply may nourish you mentally; journaling may nourish you emotionally.*

For Reflection

How often do you allow yourself to completely disconnect from technology?

What fears or beliefs keep you plugged in—and what's the worst that could happen if you unplugged?

What nourishing activity feels most appealing to you right now?

How Did It Go?

Which activity did you choose, and were you able to relax and be fully present? If so, how did you feel after doing this?

JULY 14

Challenge

Make a meal for someone—whether it's breakfast for your significant other, a sandwich to give a homeless person, or dinner for a friend.

For Reflection

When was the last time someone made a meal for you, and why did you appreciate this?

Is there someone who you know could use the food, or might appreciate not having to cook for themselves?

How might it also be an act of kindness to yourself to devote a little time to cooking, seeing it not as a chore but as a potentially rewarding experience?

How Did It Go?

What meal did you make, and for whom? What did you enjoy about the experience?

A drunk driver who I'll call Renee ran through a stop sign at an intersection, where my friend Mike Johnson was heading home from work, and crashed into his truck. He was injured so severely that he was not expected to survive. But after several surgeries and many months of physical therapy, he recovered.

Mike and his wife, Gene, not only forgave Renee, but also helped her and changed her life. She was a very young woman going down a dangerous path of partying and drinking. She was arrested after the accident, and she was terrified of going to jail when it was time for her court hearing.

Renee visited the hospital where Mike was fighting for his life. When the family noticed her there, they warmly welcomed her. Mike and Gene's adult children hugged her and told her it would be okay. They told her, "No one is perfect. We all make mistakes."

Shortly after, Renee met Gene in the hospital. She was expecting anger and hatred, but Gene hugged the girl and told her she forgave her. Renee said it was like "a 10,000-pound boulder was lifted off her." Wanting to do something to give back to the Johnsons, she organized a live music fund-raiser and raised $3,000 for them. When Mike finally recovered, he and Gene spoke on Renee's behalf at the hearing for a reduced sentence.

The kindness and forgiveness the Johnsons showed changed Renee's whole outlook and made her want to be a better person. The Johnsons consider their pain a fair price for saving Renee from killing someone else, possibly herself. They befriended her and visited her after her trial when she did go to jail. She is incarcerated for thirty-three months at a correctional facility, where she is keeping a journal to inspire other young people toward responsible life choices.

The Dalai Lama said, "Be kind whenever possible. It is always possible." It may not always be *easy*, but is indeed always possible—and it changes lives.

Reflections from JAYATI GHOSE

They were sitting on the pavement, the little boy with the black curls and the tiny girl with brown hair. They were playing a game with beads. Or was it marbles? The boy struck a row of beads with a small pebble. If he was able to scatter them, he got another shot. If he missed, the girl got a chance. They were laughing and tugging at each other. They seemed happy, though their hungry eyes and frail bodies wrapped in flimsy jackets told another story.

Aren't they cold? I wondered as I wrapped my woolen scarf tighter around my neck and walked into the warm confines of a nearby restaurant. I could still see them from the window. They were now running and rubbing their hands together to keep warm.

As I sat with my hot cup of coffee and burger, inhaling the delicious aroma, I felt a twinge of guilt. Should I offer some food to those kids? I saw a young lady walk up to them and motion them to follow her into the restaurant. She bought them a tray full of burgers with fries and Coke and made them sit at a table. The gleam in those kids' eyes at the sight of all that food was amazing. As they unwrapped their burgers and took their first hungry bites, the lady told the waiter to let them finish the meal. "Don't push them outside as soon as I leave. Let them finish eating first," she said. The waiter smiled and nodded. The lady then left.

I was awestruck at this simple act of kindness. Not only did the woman help those kids, she taught me an invaluable lesson. Kindness does not require grand gestures, big donations, or huge sacrifices. Even a small act can bring a huge smile to someone's face.

JULY 15

Challenge

Think of someone who recently made a mistake, and praise them for something they've done well to help shift their focus from their shortcomings to their strengths.

For Reflection

How has this mistake impacted this person's confidence or state of mind?

As an outside observer who loves this person, what do you understand that they may not understand at this moment?

What do you want this person to know about their capabilities and their worth?

How Did It Go?

What words of praise did you offer? Did this seem to give them a confidence boost?

JULY 16

Challenge

Watch or rewatch the video *Validation* on YouTube: http://tinybuddha.com/validation. Then follow Hugh's lead by validating everyone you encounter today.

For Reflection

Do you look for the best in others—and if not, why?

How do you feel when others see and acknowledge the best in you?

Who will you validate first today, and how?

How Did It Go?

Who did you validate today, and how? What was the most rewarding part of this challenge?

JULY 17

Challenge

Text someone who you're planning to see soon:
"I can't wait to see you on (insert day)!"

For Reflection

What do you most appreciate about this person?

What about your upcoming plans most excites you?

Why might this person appreciate a thoughtful text like this?

How Did It Go?

How do you think this tiny act may have had a big impact?

JULY 18

Challenge

Include someone who often seems lonely, whether a friend, family member, or coworker, in something you're planning to do soon.

For Reflection

Who do you know who would be touched and thrilled to receive an invitation to join you in something special you're planning to do?

Why do you think this would mean a lot to them?

How might including them make the experience even more fun and enjoyable for you?

How Did It Go?

Did this person seem excited to receive your invitation?

JULY 19

Challenge

Instead of beating yourself up over a mistake, write down one thing you learned from it and one reason you deserve to cut yourself some slack. (If you can't think of a reason, think of what your best friend would say to you.)

Mistake:

Lesson:

Why you deserve to cut yourself some slack:

How Did It Go?

Do you feel any better about yourself after shifting your perspective in this way?

JULY 20

Challenge

Leave a short uplifting note on the windshield of someone's car—something anyone would appreciate seeing at the end of a long day.

Brainstorm: *"You're beautiful, pass it on." "You're doing better than you think." "You deserve a break!"*

For Reflection

What reminder would you most appreciate, and why?

How might this affect someone's day for the better?

How Did It Go?

What did you write on the note? Did you wait around to see the person's response when they read it?

JULY 21

Challenge

When you're going to do something for yourself, ask someone else if you can do it for them as well.

Brainstorm: *Grab a coworker a coffee when you're on your break, or throw some of your roommate's dirty clothes in with your laundry.*

For Reflection

Does it naturally occur to you to do for others when you're doing things for yourself? If not, why do you think that is?

Has anyone done this for you lately? If so, how did their act of thoughtfulness make a difference in your day?

How does it affect your feelings about others when they're thoughtful in this way?

How Did It Go?

What did you end up doing or offering to do? What was the person's response?

I was driving home when I saw a man in a short-sleeved shirt wandering through our neighborhood, pushing a shopping cart. It was raining. It was unusually cold. He was walking painfully slow, and he was dripping wet.

I paused at the intersection to my street and watched him for several minutes, thinking. My heart was heavy seeing him move so slowly, so wet, so cold. I suddenly remembered I had an old trench coat that was balled up on the floor of my garage, gathering dust near the washing machine. But what if I needed it sometime in the future?

A story I had once heard at a church conference came to mind. Two boys walked down a road that led through a field. The younger of the two noticed a man toiling in the fields of his farm, his good clothes stacked neatly off to the side. The boy looked at his older friend and said, "Let's hide his shoes so when he comes from the field, he won't be able to find them. His expression will be priceless!" The boy laughed.

The older of the two boys thought for a moment and said, "The man looks poor. See his clothes? Let's do this instead: Let's hide a silver dollar in each shoe and then we'll hide in these bushes and see how he reacts to that, instead."

The younger companion agreed, so they placed a silver dollar in each shoe and hid behind the bushes. It wasn't long before the farmer came in from the field, tired and worn. He reached down and pulled on a shoe, immediately feeling the money under his foot. With the coin now between his fingers, he looked around to see who could have put it in his shoe. But no one was there. He held the dollar in his hand and stared at it in disbelief. Confused, he slid his other foot into his other shoe and felt the second coin. The man was overwhelmed when he removed the second silver dollar.

Thinking he was alone, he dropped to his knees and offered a verbal prayer that the boys could easily hear from their hiding place. They heard the poor farmer cry tears of relief and gratitude. He spoke of his sick wife and his boys in need of food. He expressed gratitude for this unexpected bounty from unknown hands.

After a time, the boys came out and slowly started their long walk home. They felt good inside, warm, changed somehow knowing the good they had done to a poor farmer in dire straits. A smile crept across their souls.

Remembering this story, I drove home, took my coat from the garage, and went looking for the old man in the rain. I spotted him. He hadn't gone far. The rain had let up some. I pulled up alongside him and asked him to come over. He hesitated and then walked closer. I asked if he had a place to stay. He said he did and was close. When I offered him my jacket, he looked stunned, like I was violating some accepted code of conduct. I urged him to take it. He slowly reached out, took my old coat, and smiled.

We all encounter poor farmers toiling in the fields of their trials and difficulties. We might not know their challenges, but their countenances often tell a story of pain. We have opportunities to hide shoes or hide silver dollars in them. This day, this time, I removed a "silver dollar" from the floor of my garage and slipped it in an old man's shoe. A life was blessed for having done it. And I think the old man's life may have been blessed by it as well.

JULY 22

Challenge

Give a warm piece of clothing that you no longer need to a homeless person, or leave it in a donation bin.

For Reflection

Is there any piece of clothing you've been holding on to in case you want it "someday" that someone else might need right now?

Do you feel comfortable handing this directly to a homeless person, and if not, why?

How might this benefit someone who feels lost, alone, and possibly hopeless?

How Did It Go?

What did you choose to part with? If you gave it directly to a homeless person, how did they respond?

JULY 23

Challenge

Send a thoughtful private message to someone who updates Facebook all the time or sends a lot of chain e-mails. They're clearly looking for connection.

For Reflection

What do you think this person's life is like, and what might it be lacking?

When was the last time you connected with them on a meaningful level?

What do you think they'd most appreciate hearing from you right now?

How Did It Go?

What did you write, and did this lead to a meaningful exchange?

JULY 24

Challenge

E-mail someone a picture you know they'd appreciate having.

Brainstorm: *For example, a picture from your childhood, a picture of a mutual friend or relative who has passed, or a picture from a shared vacation or event you both attended.*

For Reflection

Why is this particular picture meaningful to you? What feeling does this evoke?

Why might your friend appreciate having this?

How Did It Go?

What did you write in your e-mail? Did your friend appreciate that you sent this picture?

JULY 25

Challenge

As an act of kindness to your body, write below one thing you appreciate about each part you usually criticize. (If you feel inclined, you can take it one step further and say these things to your body while looking in a mirror.)

Brainstorm: *You might not love your legs, but they get you from point A to B; you might wish you had thinner arms, but they allow you to hug the people you love and hold your baby.*

Body Part You Dislike:

What You Appreciate About This:

Body Part You Dislike:

What You Appreciate About This:

Body Part You Dislike:

What You Appreciate About This:

How Did It Go?

Do you feel better able to treat your body with kindness after doing this?

JULY 26

Challenge

Put something back where it belongs instead of expecting someone else to do it.

Brainstorm: *Return a stray shopping cart in a parking lot, reshelf an item on the floor or in the wrong place at a store, return an office supply to its rightful place, or unload the dishwasher so your spouse or roommate won't have to.*

For Reflection

When you see something out of place, do you usually take the initiative to return it, or do you assume someone else will do it?

How does the simple act of returning something to its place benefit everyone around you?

How Did It Go?

What did you put away today? Who do you think benefited from this, and why?

JULY 27

Challenge

Buy something from a small local business (a coffee shop or boutique, for example), and compliment the store owner on something that makes their establishment charming or unique.

For Reflection

Are there any small local businesses in your neighborhood or town that you've always wanted to check out? Or do you have a favorite that you frequent?

If you have a favorite, why do you come back to this business time and time again?

How might your kindness improve the store owner's day?

How Did It Go?

What compliment did you offer, and how did the store owner respond?

JULY 28

Challenge

Place a bowl of candy on your desk and tell your coworkers to help themselves.

For Reflection

Do you know most of your coworkers? If not, why?

How might a small gesture like offering candy make you more available and friendly to those you work with?

Would you find it disruptive to have coworkers approaching your desk throughout the day? If so, is there another friendly gesture you could extend instead?

How Did It Go?

Did you connect with more coworkers than usual today, and was this a positive experience?

JULY 29

Challenge

Send an e-mail to someone that starts with, "I want to let you know how you've made a difference in my life." Or say it face-to-face.

For Reflection

Who has made a tremendous difference in your life and may not realize it?

What do you want them to know about what they mean to you and how they've affected your life for the better?

How would you feel if someone sent you an e-mail like this?

How Did It Go?

Did you choose to send an e-mail or say these things face-to-face? How do you think your words made a difference in their day?

JULY 30

Challenge

Surprise a loved one with something, whether it's a gift, a good deed, or a last-minute invitation to something fun and exciting.

For Reflection

Who in your life could use a surprise gesture to lift their spirits?

Based on what you know about their personality, preferences, and current challenges, what do you think they'd most enjoy right now?

Why might they appreciate this from you specifically?

How Did It Go?

Who did you surprise, and how? How do you think this made a difference in their day?

JULY 31

Challenge

Leave change near a parking meter, vending machine, or coin-operated washing machine or dryer. If you feel inclined, leave a note that reads: "This one's on me."

For Reflection

Do you feel comfortable with the idea of leaving money for someone else to find? Why or why not?

Are you less likely to do something kind if you won't be there to see the person's response? If so, why might this exercise be good for you?

How might it brighten someone's day to receive an unexpected act of thoughtfulness like this?

How Did It Go?

Where did you leave change? Did this act of thoughtfulness brighten *your* day? If so, why do you think that is?

MONTHLY REVIEW

- Which challenges were the most helpful for you, and why?
- Which challenges were the most difficult for you, and why?
- What did you learn about yourself through the process of completing these challenges?
- Did you learn anything about kindness and thoughtfulness that you didn't learn during the first month focused on these themes?
- What did you learn about the people in your life?
- Did these challenges strengthen your relationships, and how?
- Did you identify any areas for improvement and growth?
- Head over to http://tinybuddha.com/love-forums to share your experiences with other readers!

AUGUST

Acceptance and Nonjudgment

Reflections from LILY VELEZ

In college, I went out of my way to abstain from associating with people who lived their lives differently than I did. Even the smallest offenses repelled me. I would pity them for not being on my path and would figuratively shake my head in disapproval.

Then, during the second semester of my freshman year of college, I learned that the girl who lived in the dorm room next to mine had committed suicide. This was a girl who'd always been friendly with me, smiling and saying hello whenever our paths crossed. She'd also invited me to hang out with her on more than one occasion. But I'd always declined because I'd made the judgment that she and I were in different leagues.

When I heard the news about her suicide, I was instantly filled with regret and what if's—what if I'd been the friend she obviously wanted? For so many years, I'd built walls between myself and others. If they didn't see as I saw, or hear as I heard, or spoke as I spoke, or believed as I believed, I kept them at arm's length.

I've come to realize now that we are all worthy and deserving of love, and we're all hungry for it. We all want to feel validated and connected and valued. These days, I no longer judge people, because I understand that we're all on our own paths and no two paths have to be identical or completely parallel. We all have our own journeys and lessons to learn.

So, before you judge someone because they don't see as you do or behave as you do, ask yourself if your thoughts are promoting separation or love. The key to living at peace with one another is to choose love. Always.

When I was seventeen, someone robbed my grandfather as he was leaving his home. They took his car and left him on the curb, having a heart attack. He begged for help, but they didn't care. A neighbor found him there.

We were never very close to my grandfather. He cheated on my grandmother when we were young and she left him. He was never loving, and he never hugged or kissed us. What's more, I could see this distant relationship repeating itself with my father and me.

My grandfather survived the heart attack, but for a while I wasn't sure he would. I asked myself if that was the relationship I wanted to have with him. Were other people's judgments what I wanted to remember? I told my father I wanted to take the six-hour drive with him to see my grandfather. I'd never traveled with just my father, but I wanted a chance to know my grandfather better.

He was out of the hospital and back at his house, where I had never been before. I regularly went to the town where he lived but always stayed at my grandmother's because my parents didn't want us to see him with another woman. He was surprised to see me and treated me well. He asked with interest about my life. He told stories about his farm and when he was younger. I observed his sick body, his tired figure. I watched his wife take care of him.

I'm relieved and happy that I gave this relationship a chance. I put all other people's opinions of him aside and started over fresh, seeing him through my own eyes. That experience also brought me closer to my father. I could better understand the father he had and how he grew up.

I still don't have a close relationship with my grandfather, but I can say we have our *own* relationship, not influenced by anyone or based in judgment. I accept and love him the way he is. And I know the day he is gone I'll have nothing to regret.

AUGUST 1

Challenge

Write below the top three things you often judge people for, and why—what you assume about the people who have this trait or habit you're judging. Then for each, write one reason why your assumption may not be true. Keep these things in mind as you go about your day as a reminder to see people beyond your judgments.

Brainstorm: *If you often judge smokers, you may assume they're weak and selfish (because their secondhand smoke harms others). You could challenge this by recognizing that it's hard to quit an addictive behavior—even for a strong person—and that most people would never intentionally hurt others.*

1. I judge:
   I assume:
   My assumption may not be true because:
2. I judge:
   I assume:
   My assumption may not be true because:
3. I judge:
   I assume:
   My assumption may not be true because:

How Did It Go?

Did this exercise help you see people you often judge through a different lens?

AUGUST 2

Challenge

Publicly advocate for someone who others frequently judge.

Brainstorm: *If your friends frequently judge another friend who's been more negative than usual lately, try to help them understand the difficulties she's been facing; if your coworkers frequently judge another coworker who got fired for unproven allegations, let them know that no one knows the truth, and even if you did, you likely wouldn't know the whole story.*

For Reflection

Why do others judge this person so frequently and so harshly?

What fears, beliefs, or assumptions might contribute to their judgments?

What do you believe contributed to the way this person is, and what's something you can say when others begin judging?

How Did It Go?

What did you say to advocate for this person, and do you think this may have influenced anyone else's judgments?

AUGUST 3

Challenge

Identify one thing you fear people might judge you for. Keep an eye out for someone else who has this same struggle today and say something that might make them feel better about this to reinforce to both of you that neither of you deserve to be judged.

Brainstorm: *If you worry that people may judge you for your appearance because you're overweight, you could tell a heavy coworker that she looks beautiful today; if you worry people may judge you because you had children young, you could compliment another young mother on how well she seems to balance work and family.*

For Reflection

Why do you feel insecure about this and worry that people may judge you for it?

What do you wish people understood about this struggle?

How might you make a difference in someone else's day by complimenting them on something they might be insecure about?

How Did It Go?

What did you say, and how did the other person respond? Was this a rewarding experience, and if so, why?

AUGUST 4

Challenge

Think of something you've judged about your former self, and then close your eyes and forgive yourself—your *current* self—for judging that beautiful person who has always deserved love and was doing the best he or she could.

For Reflection

What do you judge most harshly about your past self, and why?

If you were viewing yourself through a lens of compassion and understanding, what would you acknowledge about why you were the way you were, or you did the things you did?

How would it change your thoughts about yourself and how you treat yourself if you always believed you were doing the best you could?

How Did It Go?

Do you view yourself any less judgmentally after completing this challenge?

AUGUST 5

Challenge

Identify someone whose past you've judged. If they're willing, ask them to tell you more about this so that you can better understand them and accept where they've come from.

For Reflection

Why have you judged this person for their past? What assumptions have you formed about them?

If you set understanding as your primary goal, what questions would you ask them?

How might understanding this person's past affect how you interact with them and improve your relationship?

How Did It Go?

Did you learn anything that helped you let go of your judgments and understand this person a little better?

AUGUST 6

Challenge

Smile and make eye contact with a stranger you're tempted to judge, and say inside your head, *I don't know your story, but I know you're a lot like me.*

For Reflection

How do you usually act around strangers you're tempted to judge?

What fears may cause you to act this way?

What kind of impact could you make on the people around you if you practiced this exercise regularly?

How Did It Go?

How did this affect your thoughts about other people? And how did other people respond?

AUGUST 7

Challenge

Whenever you're tempted to judge someone today, practice discernment instead. Through discernment, you're able to recognize which behaviors you believe are unhealthy, inappropriate, or unethical without looking down on the other person, as you would when judging.

Brainstorm: *You can discern that stealing is unethical but choose not to judge the thief, who may feel financially unable to meet her basic needs.*

For Reflection

Who in your life have you judged because of unhealthy, inappropriate, or unethical behavior?

Does it change how you perceive them to separate the person and the behavior?

How might you be able to help this person by shifting from judgment to discernment?

How Did It Go?

Were you tempted to make any judgments today, and what did you discern instead?

After my father left my mother, he and I were estranged. I had a long list of grievances that I thought proved how selfish and judgmental he was. He tore apart our family so that he could have a better life. He was harsh with his opinions about me and my siblings and used money to manipulate the situations. I wanted nothing to do with him.

After college, I decided to move to the West Coast with my boyfriend. I packed everything I owned into his Chevy truck and left for a bold adventure. We had no idea where we would go. We didn't have jobs and we barely had any money. I didn't ask my father's opinion, but I would have guessed it was disapproving.

When it was time to leave, my father brought me a gift—a Triple A card. I was stunned. To me, the card was symbolic of the gulf between us. While I followed my muse, he was practical. While I trusted fate, he prepared for the worst. While I lived on love, he thought only of money. The card was sensible when I thought that *sensible* was a bad word. I hope I thanked him but I'm not sure I did.

My boyfriend and I left for our journey, but it did not go as planned. At the Grand Canyon, we had a car accident, destroying our truck and leaving us with no way to get our belongings to California. As I began to untangle the complications of finding repair services, rental trucks, and hotels during peak tourist season, I realized that I had one valuable tool. I had Dad's Triple A card.

Dad's foresight came in handy. He had given me a deluxe card, which provided towing, a rental truck, and hotels. And when I pulled out that card and had all my needs met, it dawned on me that Dad was a pretty smart guy. He had protected me with that Triple A card. He kept me safe and gave me resources when I didn't have the common sense to have them myself. And ultimately, it was Dad who helped me finish my grand adventure.

I was surprised to realize how loving a Triple A card is. I began to understand that love comes in many forms and that I don't have the right to decide which way is right or wrong. I had judged him as harshly as he judged me. Moving across the country with no money was as ridiculous to him as his practical Triple A card was to me. But there was a key difference between us. In spite of what Dad thought, he gave me help. He protected me regardless of his opinions. And it became very clear to me that I had never done anything for him.

Now, Dad and I are close. I gladly accept his love any way he gives it, and I find it richer and more generous than I ever could have imagined. Twenty-two years after moving across the country, that same boyfriend, now father of my kids, left me. When he did, it was Dad's shoulder I cried on. I turned to him for comfort. I knew that I could count on Dad's love. I knew that he would be there for me no matter what.

AUGUST 8

Challenge

Tell someone who's angry, sad, frustrated, or stressed, "It's okay. You're allowed to feel . . ." to let them know you accept them, regardless of their emotional state, and won't judge them for feeling down.

For Reflection

Have you ever worried that others would judge you because you weren't feeling happy or positive?

How did trying to repress your emotions affect your ability to feel them, learn from them, and respond to them wisely?

How might you help your loved ones by letting them know there's nothing wrong with their emotions, and they don't have to pretend around you?

How Did It Go?

Who did you say this to today, and how did it affect them? Do you think they feel more comfortable showing you their emotions now?

AUGUST 9

Challenge

Give someone you've judged a second chance, either by starting a conversation or inviting them to join you in doing something.

For Reflection

Who in your life have you judged as selfish, rude, or something else unflattering based on your first impression? What did they do that caused you to form this judgment?

What's another possible explanation for how they acted the first time you met them?

What might you be missing by writing them off immediately? Is it worth giving them another chance?

How Did It Go?

Did this person seem any different, and are you glad you gave them a second chance?

AUGUST 10

Challenge

Avoid forming reductionist conclusions today—like "He's a jerk" or "She's a moron"—and instead, try to understand people on a deeper level.

For Reflection

What are some reductionist conclusions you've formed about people in the past to avoid trying to understand them?

Has anyone ever formed a mistaken, reductionist conclusion about you?

What would you want people to remember when they're tempted to sum you up in this way?

How Did It Go?

Were you able to look a little deeper today? How did this affect your interactions?

AUGUST 11

Challenge

Identify one to three of your biggest flaws and write below all the ways these have served you well to help you foster greater self-acceptance, in spite of your imperfection.

Brainstorm: *For example, your impatience may help you be persistent, enabling you to do well in your career; and your sensitivity may contribute to your power as a performer.*

Flaw:

How this serves you well:

Flaw:

How this serves you well:

Flaw:

How this serves you well:

How Did It Go?

Did this help you feel any differently about your flaws? How might it affect your actions if you remembered these things going forward?

AUGUST 12

Challenge

Ask someone to tell you more about one of their interests, habits, or beliefs that you often judge.

For Reflection

Why do you judge this interest, belief, or habit?

Have you assumed anything about this interest, belief, or habit that may not be true? What would help you keep an open mind?

How many people do you think you've closed yourself off to as a result of holding this judgment?

How Did It Go?

What did you learn, and do you feel any differently about this person as a result?

AUGUST 13

Challenge

Identify someone in your life you regularly try to change. Now identify one thing you appreciate about them, just as they are—and share this with them.

For Reflection

Why do you frequently try to change this person?

What do you hope to gain in doing this, and what do you lose?

What would this relationship be like if you both accepted each other fully and completely as you are?

How Did It Go?

What did you share with them, and how did they respond? Did sharing this help you focus more on what you like about them and less on what you dislike?

AUGUST 14

Challenge

Choose a loved one you regularly judge. Now do something small but thoughtful to show them you love and care about them, in spite of your judgment.

For Reflection

Has your judgment ever prevented you from treating this person with kindness and consideration?

Why do you love this person, and when was the last time you showed or told them?

Based on what you know about their personality and lifestyle, what do you think would be the most helpful thing you could do for them today?

How Did It Go?

What did you choose to do? Was this difficult for you? Why or why not?

Last year, I was on the subway, during rush hour, heading to class to take an exam. After making my usual transfer to another train line, I was able to find a free seat. I acknowledged the woman sitting near me just enough to immediately write her off as someone I wanted to ignore. She looked at me and smiled, and I gave a half smile back but turned slightly away to make it clear that I didn't want to chat.

I am a warm person, hardly ever without a smile, and usually very open, but I was having a day where I just felt disinterested in others, and the last thing I wanted was to feel trapped in a conversation with a "lowly" woman on the train who might pester me for money. I pulled out my textbook, wallet in hand, to begin "reviewing" for my exam. She began engaging me in small talk, and, after a few minutes, my disposition changed. My short answers became longer, and I became genuinely interested in what she had to say.

I got off the train feeling lighthearted after she told me a bit about her life. We had a short but beautiful conversation. After walking the couple of blocks to class, I realized I had left my wallet on the train. Well played. "Distract someone with small talk in hopes they'll leave something behind," a peer commented when I retold the story.

My professor excused me, and I headed back to the station. When I explained that I'd forgotten my wallet, they informed me that a woman had notified a subway employee—just as the train left the station where I'd gotten off—that someone had left one on the train, and that I'd gotten off at the specific stop.

I rode the train to its last stop where all the lost and found items are dropped. When I claimed my wallet, everything was inside. I learned that day not to prejudge someone's character because of their appearance, and to always be open because you never know what good will come from it.

I felt about an inch tall when I found out a friend didn't tell me something important that had happened in her life because she feared I would judge her. Did all my friends feel this way? Why? I've always felt very protective of them and tried my best to be a great friend.

I'm an only child. I've spent a lot of time with my parents. They're wonderful and they've done a lot for me, but one thing they've passed on is a sort of judgmental, sarcastic type of humor. I catch myself gossiping and talking about others, essentially judging them. I'll admit there are times when I feel as if I'm better than someone. But who am I to think that? I've made mistakes. I don't always do or say the right things. I'm by no means perfect or better than anyone else.

Suddenly, I understood what my friend meant. Even though I hoped she knew that I would never judge her choices and I'd always be there for her, I could see why she was afraid to tell me. I didn't want to define myself as a judgmental person who people couldn't trust to talk about important issues, so I vowed to change.

Why do we judge others anyway? I think it stems partly from how we were raised to think and speak, but it also stems from our own insecurities.

This incident taught me to be more compassionate and it reminded me that everyone has flaws. I also realized that people make decisions that feel right for them, even if they wouldn't be right for me. And sometimes they make their choice because of something I don't know anything about.

It's human nature to compare ourselves to others and question their choices and decisions. But we are only accountable for our own lives. Judging other people can hurt relationships, like it hurt mine. We can define ourselves as judgmental or compassionate through our actions and reactions. Which would *you* rather be?

AUGUST 15

Challenge

Spend five minutes people-watching today and mentally compliment everyone you see instead of forming judgments about them.

For Reflection

How often do you judge strangers for their appearance or behavior?

How do these judgments affect how you engage with and respond to strangers?

If people were to judge you on a quick impression like this, how far would they be from knowing your whole, true self?

How Did It Go?

Were you tempted to form any judgments? What kind of compliments did you come up with?

AUGUST 16

Challenge

Identify one behavior or lifestyle choice you regularly judge, then google this and read an article that helps you understand it a little better.

For Reflection

Why do you judge this behavior or lifestyle choice?

How do you treat people who do this as a result, and does that reflect the kind of person you want to be?

Do you think it would help you be more understanding if you had more information about it? Why or why not?

How Did It Go?

What's one thing you learned in googling that can help you develop a greater sense of acceptance for people who do this or make this choice?

AUGUST 17

Challenge

Identify someone who recently made a choice that you've judged. Start a friendly conversation about this choice—in person or in an e-mail—both to learn more about why they chose this and to show them you accept them and their choices.

For Reflection

Why have you judged this choice?

How has your judgment affected your relationship?

What would you do differently in this relationship if you weren't holding this judgment, and how might this affect the other person in a positive way?

How Did It Go?

Did you learn anything about this person or their choice that you didn't know before? Do you feel less judgmental as a result?

AUGUST 18

Challenge

Recognize when you're about to form a judgment today, then do something to help that person instead of looking down on them.

Brainstorm: *If you're tempted to judge someone who just snapped at her child, you could ask compassionately how she's been feeling lately and then share how yoga has helped you create a sense of inner calm; if you're tempted to judge someone who frequently complains about his job but never looks for a different one, you could instead connect him with a friend whose company is hiring.*

For Reflection

Has anyone ever helped you when they could easily have judged you instead?

How did this make a difference in your life?

What would the world be like if we all committed to helping each other instead of judging each other?

How Did It Go?

Who did you help today, and how? How do you think this made a positive difference for them?

AUGUST 19

Challenge

Identify one thing you've been striving to change. Now write this down: "Even though I am working to change ________________, I completely and unconditionally accept myself where I am right now." Read this several times throughout the day.

For Reflection

How have you treated yourself because of this thing you want to change?

Why do you deserve love and acceptance, in spite of this thing you have been striving to change? (If you're not sure, think of something a loved one might say about you.)

How might it actually help you create change to foster a greater sense of self-acceptance?

How Did It Go?

Did this help you foster a greater sense of self-acceptance? Would you be open to doing this regularly to see how it could affect you over time?

AUGUST 20

Challenge

Eliminate the word *should* from your vocabulary today to help you foster greater acceptance and judge others—and yourself—less.

For Reflection

How do you feel about yourself when you tell yourself (or others tell you) that you should or shouldn't think, feel, or do something?

What's your intention when you use the word *should* in regards to yourself or others, and in what ways has this backfired in the past?

How would it benefit you and your relationships to stop *should*ing all over yourself and others?

How Did It Go?

Did this help you judge less and accept more? Did anything positive happen as a result?

AUGUST 21

Challenge

Make this your mantra today: "My way isn't better; it's just different. It isn't right; it's just right for me."

For Reflection

Can you think a time when you assumed that your way was the right way and pushed it on someone else?

How did this affect your relationship?

How might this person have felt if you'd adopted—and acted on—this mantra?

How Did It Go?

Did you feel more accepting of different ways of doing things? If so, how did you act as a result, and how did this affect your interactions?

For years after I moved out of my parents' home, each visit back would be preceded by careful, specific preparation. I would try to brace myself for whatever would be coming my way. I would spend the entire two-hour bus ride turning all the possible criticisms and probable arguments over and over in my head. I would rehearse ways I could react to various imagined scenarios. I thought preparing myself would soften the blows. It didn't.

Imagine my embarrassment and hopelessness at thinking I'd finally cracked the secrets of peace and happiness, only to find myself welling up with the same old anger and resentment each time I faced my closest relatives. Even after I began a journey of personal and spiritual growth, visits back home were toxic. I would prepare. I'd show up. They would judge me. I'd react. Then I would judge myself for letting their judgment get to me. Then they'd judge me for letting it get to me. Then I'd judge them for judging me. It would be a giant, exhausting mess.

One day, in the midst of recovering from such a visit, I found myself in an intimate conversation with a friend about beauty. She shared with me how she sometimes felt so disgusted by her reflection that she could hardly function. I empathized, letting her know that I had suffered with that severity of self-hatred for close to ten years.

I said, "You know what I've learned? It wasn't my reflection that was hurting me. It was my expectation that, every time I looked in the mirror, I would discover someone else, some other person who wasn't me. Jennifer Aniston maybe? But Jennifer Aniston never showed up. It was always just the same old me. That was what really hurt—the expectation was never met."

Immediately after the words poured out of my mouth, my mind lit on fire. I realized, with stark clarity, that the same relationship I used to have with my reflection, I was having with my parents. I kept showing up, time after time, expecting different people to magically appear. I kept expecting that they would change. I thought about my relationship with myself, and how I'd heard messages of self-love, self-acceptance, and self-forgiveness, but it took me years to truly internalize them. Maybe that's how it was with my parents. It wasn't that I didn't know the answer. I just had to be ready to experience it.

The next time I went home, it was like a whole new world. I didn't brace myself for criticism, nor did I plan my words. I just showed up with the assumption that maybe they would never change. This simple belief completely transformed my relationship with them. Suddenly, I could see them for who they were. They were, and always will be, flawed and beautiful, just like me. I could suddenly smile at their criticism and laugh at their judgment. I could embrace them even if they didn't feel like embracing me. I could understand them even if they misunderstood me.

I used to think that people who had good relationships with their parents had perfect parents. That's just not true. People who get along with their parents have just as many family conflicts as anyone else. They just choose to accept those conflicts as part of life, and love their kin anyway. Of course, it's not easy. Nothing worth having is easy, but it's always simple. And this is my simple message, today and forever: accept and allow. That is the path toward peace, love, and serenity.

AUGUST 22

Challenge

Identify one thing you've learned from knowing a person whom you regularly judge, even if it's just an opportunity to practice being open-minded. Share this at tinybuddha.com /love-forums to start a conversation that may help others.

For Reflection

Why is this lesson valuable, and how might your life and relationships improve if you applied it?

How can you start applying this lesson in your life and relationships now?

Does it change your perception of this person to consider that they've given you this gift?

How Did It Go?

What lesson did you identify, and could anyone in the community forums relate?

AUGUST 23

Challenge

Practice the Japanese art of wabi-sabi, and look for something imperfect but beautiful to place somewhere you'll see it often. Whenever you look at this, remind yourself that we are all like this item—imperfect, yet unique and beautiful.

Brainstorm: *It could be the ceramic mug your child made for you, the chipped picture frame that you found in an antique shop, or a sparse bouquet of flowers that called to you like Charlie Brown's wilting Christmas tree.*

For Reflection

Do you own anything that's imperfect but beautiful? Why do you see beauty in this?

How might it change your relationships if you looked for beauty in people's imperfections?

How would it change your life if other people found beauty in yours?

How Did It Go?

Did you perceive others differently as a result of this exercise?

AUGUST 24

Challenge

Put a quarter in a jar whenever you criticize someone today or think a critical or judgmental thought. At the end of the day, give this money to a homeless person, and choose to view them compassionately, without judgment.

For Reflection

The last few times you criticized people in your life, what was your positive intention?

Did your criticism have the desired effect, and if not, what happened instead?

How might you be able to act on your intentions without being critical?

How Did It Go?

Did this help you curb the instinct to be critical and judgmental? How much money did you put aside?

AUGUST 25

Challenge

Be antigossip today. Whenever anyone talks about anyone else, change the subject to something positive about that person.

For Reflection

Who and what do you usually gossip about?

What underlying need drives the urge to gossip? To feel better about yourself? To connect with others? To vent about someone toward whom you feel resentment?

What would be a healthier way to meet that need?

How Did It Go?

Did you feel the urge to gossip today? If so, what positive thing did you say instead?

AUGUST 26

Challenge

Identify something you often judge in others that you do, as well. Realize that you likely judge your loved one so harshly *because* you've done this, too—and the guiltier you feel about it, the stronger your judgments will be. Now write a short letter to both of you, empathizing with why you both do this, and offering love and acceptance in spite of your imperfections and struggles.

Dear self and ______________,

How Did It Go?

Did you form any helpful new insights in writing this letter?

AUGUST 27

Challenge

Whenever you think about something you believe someone else should change or do differently, shift the focus back to yourself and identify something *you* could change or do differently—and act on it.

Brainstorm: *If you think your coworker should work harder because you work ten-hour days, you could recognize that you're pushing yourself too hard and choose to ask someone else for help.*

For Reflection

In which relationships do you focus on what you think the other people should do differently?

How does this negatively impact those relationships?

How might your life and those relationships improve if you identified instead where your power lies—and used it?

How Did It Go?

Who did you think about changing today, and how did you flip your focus back to yourself?

AUGUST 28

Challenge

Fill in the blank: "When I'm striving for perfection, I often treat myself poorly by ________________." Now identify one positive, self-affirming thing you can do when you feel the instinct to do this, and utilize this when relevant today.

Brainstorm: *If you push yourself to do too much, you could choose to stop and take a walk while breathing deeply instead; if you criticize your efforts in your head, you could choose to look yourself in the mirror and say "You're doing a great job" instead.*

For Reflection

Would you ever treat anyone else this way because they didn't do something perfectly?

How do you feel as a result of this poor treatment, and how does it affect your thoughts and actions?

How might it affect your state of mind—and how would that affect the rest of your life—if you chose to do something self-affirming instead of treating yourself poorly?

How Did It Go?

What self-affirming activity did you choose, and how did you feel after doing this?

AUGUST 29

Challenge

Whenever someone criticizes themselves today, counter that with praise.

For Reflection

What fears, beliefs, feelings, or insecurities often lead you to criticize yourself?

What are you hoping to accomplish when you criticize yourself—and does it actually work?

How might you make a difference in other people's lives by helping them shift their focus from what they think they're doing wrong to what they're doing right?

How Did It Go?

What praise did you offer today, and did this seem to help?

AUGUST 30

Challenge

Identify one negative, inaccurate thing people could assume about you based on your weakest moment. Bring this to mind whenever you're tempted to judge others today, and consider that maybe you're not seeing *them*, but rather one of their weakest moments.

For Reflection

Are you quick to define others based on isolated incidents—and why or why not?

What's something negative that people could assume about you based on your weakest moment?

Why was this one moment not representative of who you are as a person?

How Did It Go?

Did this help you see people through a wider, less judgmental lens?

AUGUST 31

Challenge

Identify one physical characteristic that often leads you to form judgments or assumptions about people, whether it's a hairstyle, a style of dressing, or even a certain ethnicity. Go out of your way to start a conversation with someone who has this physical characteristic today to challenge your assumptions.

For Reflection

What assumptions have you formed based on this characteristic, and have you ever met someone with this characteristic who surprised you?

How do you act around people with this characteristic as a result of your assumptions? Has anyone ever acted like this around you? If so, how did you feel as a result?

What are some assumptions people could form about *you* based on your appearance, and has anyone ever judged you because of this?

How Did It Go?

What did you talk about? Was the conversation surprising in any way?

MONTHLY REVIEW

- Which challenges were the most helpful for you, and why?
- Which challenges were the most difficult for you, and why?
- What did you learn about yourself through the process of completing these challenges? Did you form any new insights about releasing judgments and fostering acceptance?
- What did you learn about the people in your life?
- Did these challenges strengthen your relationships, and how?
- Did you identify any areas for improvement and growth?
- Head over to http://tinybuddha.com/love-forums to share your experiences with other readers!

SEPTEMBER

Releasing Comparisons and Competition

Reflections from MICHELLE FAUST-DAVIS

While attending the wedding of a high school friend, I ran into a classmate I had not seen in several years. A brilliant student who graduated at the top of our class, she was an accomplished musician who won several awards for her achievements. After attending an elite college, she moved to New York City and held a very secure and respectable job. Of course, I knew all this thanks to the many hours I spent on Facebook.

She asked me what I had been up to. This was my worst nightmare! I had nothing impressive to say. No one would recognize the name of the small town I was living in. I didn't have a fancy job or a prestigious title. In fact, I had no idea what I was doing with my life.

I replied almost apologetically, "Well, I just moved to New Mexico and I guess, ummm, I'm still trying to figure things out." I was eager to change the subject.

"Tell me about living in New York City—how exciting!" I gushed. I imagined that surely she was living the glamorous big-city life, going to trendy bars with her favorite girlfriends after work and hanging out in Central Park on the weekends.

"Well," she replied, "I'm usually too tired after work to go out, so I normally stay in and watch TV." I was surprised by her answer, but pleased with her candor.

As we continued talking, I casually mentioned I had recently adopted a cat from an animal shelter. Her face lit up. "I wish I could have a cat, but my apartment is too small and it's too expensive for me to have one right now. You're so lucky!"

I was floored! Here I was in awe of her success, while she was making a fuss over my feline companion. We chatted more about our shared affection for animals, while my feelings of inferiority started to fade away.

When I start feeling the need to compare myself with other people, I remind myself of that encounter. If we had both kept our defenses up, our desire to compete would have prevented our opportunity to connect.

Reflections from HANNAH BRAIME

Recently, I was talking with a couple of friends about how things were going in our respective businesses. One of them shared that she had just had her best month yet and earned more than ever before. I was simultaneously happy for her and deeply envious. I had been working really hard and, although I felt good about how things were going, I compared how much I was earning to how much she was earning and found myself falling seriously short.

On an intellectual level, I rationalized that money wasn't everything, but on an emotional level I entered a comparison-based downward spiral. I started questioning what I was doing wrong, feeling self-doubt, and digging myself into a pit that left me with a general sense that I wasn't "enough."

I recognized that this wasn't serving me and spoke to my life coach about the experience. When I explained that I couldn't even imagine making that much and that I was wondering how she had done that herself, he asked, "Did you ask her?"

As soon as he asked the question, it seemed like such an obvious thing to do. But I hadn't—because I had felt ashamed. In that moment, my ego-based comparison had robbed me of the opportunity to learn, to be inspired, and to grow.

When we compare ourselves to others, it's usually because they have something, are doing something, or being something that we want to have, do, or be. When we notice that, and notice that uncomfortable feeling of envy arising, we have a decision to make: we can beat ourselves up over the gap between where we are and where they are, or we can ask ourselves *What is this comparison telling me about what I'm wanting/needing right now?* and *What can I learn from this person to get myself closer to where I want to be?*

SEPTEMBER 1

Challenge

Think of something a friend has achieved and what you admire or envy about this. Now use this as inspiration; identify a goal you're passionate or excited about and take one tiny step toward this today. (Bonus—share with your friend how they've inspired you.)

For Reflection

Are you more likely to feel inspired or envious when someone achieves something impressive? If you chose the latter, why do you think that is?

Do you believe you are just as capable as the people in your life? If not, why, and what could you do (or stop doing) to increase your confidence?

How does it affect your relationships when you work toward your goals and feel good about your efforts and yourself as a result?

How Did It Go?

What tiny step did you take today, and how did you feel after doing this? Did you share this with the person who inspired you?

SEPTEMBER 2

Challenge

Identify someone who has done something you'd like to do, and then e-mail that person for advice instead of comparing and despairing.

For Reflection

What's prevented you from doing this thing you've wanted to do?

Have you asked this person for advice before, and if not, why? What thoughts, fears, or beliefs have gotten in your way?

What questions could you ask them to help you make progress toward your goal?

How Did It Go?

Did you receive a response? If so, did you learn anything that makes you feel better able to move forward instead of getting stuck in comparisons and envy?

SEPTEMBER 3

Challenge

Share this quote on one of your social media pages, or write it in your e-mail signature: "*The reason we struggle with insecurity is because we compare our behind-the-scenes with everyone else's highlight reel.*" ~Steve Furtick

For Reflection

What types of things have you felt bad about when comparing yourself to your social media connections?

What assumptions have you formed about their lives and yours?

Does it change your feelings to consider that everyone does this, and everyone can appreciate this quote—even those you believe have "better" lives than you?

How Did It Go?

Did anyone comment on this quote? What did they say?

SEPTEMBER 4

Challenge

Write down three ways you're fortunate, and read this list before speaking with anyone you envy or think is better than you today.

Ways You're Fortunate:

1.

2.

3.

How Did It Go?

Did remembering how you're fortunate help you focus less on other people's blessings and more on your own?

SEPTEMBER 5

Challenge

Identify a friend who may feel "behind" in life, and then share something you admire or respect about where they are right now.

For Reflection

Why do you think this person feels "behind" in life, when it comes to the milestones they've reached?

What life choices have led to their current circumstances, and why were these wise choices for them?

What helps you when you're feeling behind in any aspect of your life?

How Did It Go?

What did you share? Do you think you helped this person feel better about where they are in life?

SEPTEMBER 6

Challenge

Identify a friend or colleague who shares similar goals as you, and share something useful you've learned that will help them instead of trying to get ahead of them.

For Reflection

Has anyone done this for you before? If so, how did it make a positive difference in your life?

Are you aware of any specific struggles this person is facing on the path to their goals?

Are these struggles you've faced before? If so, what do you wish you knew back then?

How Did It Go?

What lesson did you share? Did it seem to help?

SEPTEMBER 7

Challenge

Publicly congratulate someone you see as a competitor for an achievement.

For Reflection

What has this person achieved, and why is this admirable?

Do you feel personally motivated to offer congratulations? If not, why?

What would you need to do for yourself to be in the right headspace to celebrate their success?

How Did It Go?

When and where did you offer congratulations? How did this person respond?

Our culture is obsessed with winning. At school we learn that we have to compete to get what we want. Many of us grow up internalizing this idea and subtly infusing it into our relationships, friendships, career, and even spiritual path. If this is a strong trait for us, we can carry around a pervading sense of alienation, disconnectedness, or even mistrust.

In my early days as a Buddhist monk, I remember being shocked when I began to see that in the quietude of my mind, in this harmless, benevolent environment, I was secretly measuring myself and others according to how "spiritual" we were. I was trying to be the best. I was doing many things, some of them ridiculous in hindsight, to be seen as better than others. The flip side of this was that I never felt good enough. Our fixation with winning is an attempt to cover up the feeling of being somehow deficient.

A couple years ago I met an old friend who asked me what I was doing these days. I replied, somewhat mischievously, "Being a bit of a loser."

He looked confused. Then he looked sad for me. Then he asked, "You're joking, right?"

"Well, kind of . . ."

Obviously being a loser can mean all kinds of things, and most of them aren't states to be desired! But I find it fun to explore this in a Buddhist context, where winning and losing are seen as just different sides of the same coin. They never ultimately satisfy, nor can they ever ultimately degrade one's value.

When I ask myself if I can be okay with being a bit of a loser, it's tongue-in-cheek. But it holds a clear mirror up to the part of the heart that's always looking for the next thing, scheming about a future, and generating crowds of a nebulous "them" who are cheering me on, or muttering their disapproval. In other words, delusion! Allowing the heart to let go and lose a little goes a long way in releasing us from these forces of worry, drivenness, self-aversion, disconnectedness, and alienation.

My father died recently from complications of idiopathic pulmonary fibrosis (IPF). It is, by far, the deepest sorrow I have ever experienced. Dad and I had a special bond, and so in his death I lost not only a father, but a teacher, a counselor, an intellectual sparring partner, and a friend.

At his viewing and funeral, I became fascinated, if not perplexed, by the things that people said in an attempt to comfort me. While I found some phrases bizarre (especially the "He looks great" one), I understood they were spoken out of compassion and I found comfort in them. I also realized that most people were there because of their relationship with Dad and were coming to terms with their own grief.

The most confounding responses, however, were the word choices that set up a competition—a so-called suffering Olympics—of grief. These conversations went in one of two directions: either the person told me how his/her grief was worse than mine, or it went to the opposite extreme with the person saying that his/her own grief was insignificant in comparison to mine.

I was stunned by these interactions. The more I reflected on these conversations, the more I realized that grief is immeasurable. We are all unique, as are our relationships with others. If uniqueness means that each individual's experience is unlike any other, then we cannot compare ours against theirs—there simply is no comparison. Grief is not a competition, and to make it one involves minimizing someone's pain and loss.

Despite the unique ways we experience them, grief and loss are universally experienced and connect us to one another. In short, they make us human. When we compete or try to "one-up" each other's suffering, we only add pain and squander an opportunity to give to others in need, and even deny ourselves, the love and compassion to which we are all entitled.

SEPTEMBER 8

Challenge

Write down how you believe our society defines "winning" in life, and then write down how you personally define success. Whenever you feel bad about yourself today because someone else seems closer to the first definition, remind yourself of the second.

How Did It Go?

Did you need this reminder today? If so, did this help you feel better about your choices and circumstances, and less likely to compare yourself to others?

SEPTEMBER 9

Challenge

Let someone else pass you on the road today instead of battling to stay ahead. If you don't drive, let someone else go ahead of you during your commute.

For Reflection

Do you ever see driving as a race or get frustrated when others get ahead of you?

How much time do you actually gain in rushing to stay ahead of other people?

What might you gain if you drove calmly, not competitively, and what might you give to the people sharing the road with you?

How Did It Go?

Did you feel different driving today? Was your commute less stressful, and do you think you made it more pleasant for others?

SEPTEMBER 10

Challenge

Make it a goal not to one-up anyone today.

Brainstorm: *Examples of one-upping: "You've been struggling with infertility for a year? It's been four for me!" And "You only slept five hours last night? Try working on three!"*

For Reflection

When was the last time you engaged in this type of conversation with someone?

What did you hope to convey or gain in doing this?

How could you have met these needs without creating a sense of competition?

How Did It Go?

Were you tempted to one-up anyone today? If so, what did you say instead?

SEPTEMBER 11

Challenge

Whenever you're tempted to brag today—in person or on your social media pages—ask yourself if you're looking to feel worthy or significant and think about what you're hoping to hear from the other person. Then say that thing to yourself instead of bragging.

For Reflection

Do you ever find yourself bragging to prove you're significant or bolster your self-confidence?

What type of response do you hope to receive from others when you brag about your life or accomplishments?

What would you need to believe about yourself to be less dependent on this kind of feedback—and if you don't believe this about yourself, why?

How Did It Go?

Were you tempted to brag today? What were you hoping to hear, and how did you feel when you said this to yourself?

SEPTEMBER 12

Challenge

Recognize when you're tempted to "knock someone down a peg" because they seem arrogant and boastful. Instead, empathize with their desire to feel significant and build them up with a few words of praise, support, or encouragement.

For Reflection

What are things you've thought or felt about people who seemed arrogant or boastful in the past?

How have you responded to this type of behavior?

What are some reasons they might act in this way? Can you relate?

How Did It Go?

Were you able to see arrogant, boastful people through a more compassionate lens?

SEPTEMBER 13

Challenge

Keep track of tiny victories today to keep you focused on your own accomplishments, however small. (Bonus: Ask a friend or two to share their most recent tiny victories so they can reap the benefits of this challenge, as well.)

Brainstorm: *For example, getting the kids to school on time, writing a page of the book you're working on, making a half-court shot, or cooking a great meal.*

For Reflection

When was the last time you stopped to recognize and celebrate a tiny victory?

How might you feel about yourself if you always acknowledged even your tiniest accomplishments?

How might it affect your instinct to compare if you regularly felt good about yourself and your efforts—and how might that affect your relationships?

How Did It Go?

What tiny victories did you celebrate today? Why are these tiny things really big things?

SEPTEMBER 14

Challenge

Whenever you compare yourself to someone who seems to have it worse than you (a downward comparison) and feel better about yourself as a result, remember that person is likely comparing themselves to you (an upward comparison) and, consequently, feeling bad about themselves. Then compliment that person on something to help them remember they aren't "less than" because of their struggle.

For Reflection

Have you ever felt better about yourself after comparing yourself to someone who seems to have it worse than you?

How do you feel about yourself when *you're* the person who seems to have it worse?

What would you want to hear in that moment when you're feeling inferior to others?

How Did It Go?

Did you make any downward comparisons today? If so, what compliment did you offer, and did the other person seem to appreciate your effort?

At twenty-two years old, I felt lost in the world. Though I'd studied acting and writing in college, I'd missed my graduation after spending months hospitalized for an eating disorder. Then, with dwindling confidence and no sense of direction, I'd gotten a full-time job in social services and a weekend gig promoting the *Boston Globe*.

Every Saturday and Sunday morning, I stood outside a subway station alongside a homeless newspaper vendor named Lou. My job was to draw attention to us with unbridled enthusiasm. I took pride in generating more sales for our stop than the others in the area, especially since he earned more if we sold more. Also, I found it personally satisfying to be far perkier than anyone would expect a papergirl to be at 6:00 A.M. on a cold autumn morning.

I'd scream, "Extra! Extra!" and share the day's headline, then shout, "Read all about it!" I'd point at commuters and say, "Hey you—*yes you*! Did you know the *Globe* costs less than the *Herald*?" I'd hop around shouting, "Brrr—it's cold! Why not get a hot cup of coffee and then settle in with the *Globe*!" Sales increased by more than 300 percent, and my employer frequently praised my efforts. While I could convince myself to do almost anything if I got approval for it, I stuck with this because I enjoyed it. I felt good about brightening the morning for people, and through something as simple as selling a newspaper outside the subway.

One morning, I saw a former college classmate walking directly toward me. She'd also studied acting, though, unlike me, she'd received admission the first time she auditioned, and she'd actually made it to graduation. She was dressed impeccably in something fashionable and trendy. I, on the other hand, was wearing an oversize sweatshirt underneath a *Boston Globe* sandwich board. I felt completely exposed and inferior, and terrified of being judged.

She saw me and asked what my plans were going forward—after she told me she planned to move to New York and audition, as I'd always dreamed of doing. I wanted her to know I hadn't failed in life, and I had just as much potential as her. Except I wasn't sure I believed it. She was tall and toned; I was short and mushy. She was confident and outgoing; I was insecure and a loner. But most alarming to me, she was talented enough to really make it, whereas my talents seemed best suited to street-side promotions.

I wished I could be her—to have all her strengths, skills, and possibilities. Since I couldn't have that, I decided I'd settle for her validation. I considered telling her I was finding my way, and I enjoyed what I was doing, so it wasn't as bad as it looked. But instead I just said, "Wow, the crowd's getting big! Got to go—we'll catch up soon!" Which, of course, never happened, since I never saw her again.

Suddenly, I went from energized and engaged to deflated and disconnected. After ten minutes of whimpering to commuters, "Here, take a *Globe*," I looked over at Lou, still doing what he always did. And I realized I was letting him down. I might not have felt important, but what I did was important to him. When I wasn't worrying about who I thought was better than me, I felt better about myself, did better for the people around me, and was better able to make the best of what I was doing. I could either focus on my perceived weaknesses or continue using my strengths. I had a feeling that choosing the latter would increase my odds of finding my way in life. Equally important, it would improve my ability to enjoy the moment and engage with the people around me. And really, isn't that what we all want?

Sure, we also want growth and fulfillment, and we can have those things if we work at them. But I suspect we worry that other people are better than us because we want to feel worthy of connection and happiness. Though I've needed to remind myself often, I now know the key is to *believe* we are worthy—regardless of what we've achieved—and to act like it.

SEPTEMBER 15

Challenge

Before engaging with others, spend two minutes standing with your back straightened, your hands on your hips, and your chin lifted. According to psychologist and Harvard Business School professor Amy Cuddy, "power posing" can create a 20 percent increase in testosterone and a 25 percent decrease in the stress hormone cortisol, resulting in an increased feeling of confidence. Take this energy into your actions to remind you that you're no less worthy than anyone else.

For Reflection

When talking to others, are you more likely to hunch your shoulders and cross your arms, or stand straight with open body language?

How does this affect your state of mind and how you interact with others?

How do you think others perceive you based on your body language?

How Did It Go?

How did "power posing" affect your state of mind? Did you feel any different in your interactions today?

SEPTEMBER 16

Challenge

Instead of trying to be better than others, identify one way you can be better today than you were yesterday—and act on it.

Brainstorm: *If you didn't make time for your passion project yesterday, you could prioritize it today; if you snapped at a loved one yesterday, you could apologize today.*

For Reflection

In what area of your life have you made comparisons lately, and why?

How do you feel, physically and mentally, when focusing on what others are doing?

How does this affect your ability to make improvements in your own life?

How Did It Go?

What improvement did you make, and how did you feel as a result?

SEPTEMBER 17

Challenge

Write down three of your top strengths. If you're tempted to compare yourself with someone else today, refer to this list as a reminder that we all have our own strengths and weaknesses.

Your Top Strengths:

1.

2.

3.

How Did It Go?

Did identifying your strengths help you minimize comparisons? How did this affect your interactions with others?

SEPTEMBER 18

Challenge

Compliment someone on a trait they possess that you would like to cultivate.

For Reflection

What do you find admirable about this trait?

How might it temper your envy to use this as an opportunity for connection and appreciation?

Why do you want to cultivate this in yourself—and how can you start today?

How Did It Go?

What compliment did you offer, and how did it feel to build someone up?

SEPTEMBER 19

Challenge

Avoid something that usually triggers comparisons all day today.

Brainstorm: *For example, social media, fashion magazines, or specific reality TV shows.*

For Reflection

How does it usually affect your state of mind when you devote time to one of these triggers?

How do you feel about yourself, and how do you act as a result?

How might your life and relationships improve if you minimized exposure to these triggers?

How Did It Go?

How did it feel to remove this influence? Might you do this more often going forward?

SEPTEMBER 20

Challenge

Identify a relationship that you frequently compare unfavorably to someone else's relationship (for example, someone else's relationship with their husband or mother). Now shift your focus back to your own relationship and identify one tiny thing you could do to strengthen it.

Brainstorm: *If you envy someone whose mother is her best friend, you could invite your mother to join you for lunch to strengthen your relationship. If you envy someone whose wife frequently does small thoughtful things, you could do something thoughtful for your wife to set the tone for a more giving relationship.*

For Reflection

What do you envy about this person's relationship?

How can you take responsibility for improving your own relationship so it's stronger, even if not perfect?

How might your relationship improve if you stopped romanticizing other people's relationships and focused on what you can control?

How Did It Go?

What did you do to strengthen your relationship? Do you feel it made a difference?

SEPTEMBER 21

Challenge

Invite someone to do something competitive so you can practice releasing your attachment to winning and being a gracious winner or loser.

Brainstorm: *You could go bowling, play minigolf, or play a board game.*

For Reflection

Do you usually focus on fun, winning, or both when doing a competitive activity with others?

Do you find these activities less enjoyable if you don't win?

Do you think people enjoy doing competitive activities with you? If not, why, and how can you work on this?

How Did It Go?

What competitive activity did you choose? Were you able to enjoy the activity without focusing on winning?

I was talking with a friend about her marriage when she confessed that she was once a scorekeeper. She used to keep a mental tally of what she had done and what her husband hadn't, and she gave a whole lot of meaning to that score. When I asked how she came to leave the score keeping behind, she told me that her husband said something one day that completely turned it around for her.

In the midst of one of her score reports, her husband said the reason he never thought that way was because he saw them as a team. She gives more in some ways and he gives more in other ways, but why keep track when they are always working together, in the end? She instantly knew that was true. He did give more than her in many ways, but her rigid, defensive outlook hadn't allowed her to even notice what he did for her.

She never looked at her relationship in quite the same way again. When she found herself feeling wronged, she remembered that she and her husband were teammates, not adversaries.

When you're focused on yourself, keeping score, and making sure you're being treated properly, you're not actually in relationship with another person—you're in relationship with *your thoughts* about the other person. You're focusing on yourself, what you can get, and where your partner is falling short. Thinking of the two of you as a team shifts your focus. Suddenly it's not "me versus you"; it's "us."

It's no longer "I did the laundry every day this week, what did you do?" It's "We're a team. I do the laundry more than you at times, and you do a million other things for me at times."

Even if you aren't a scorekeeper always looking for where you were wronged, taking on the team viewpoint can bring a new sense of closeness to your relationships. Can you imagine what might happen if we extended this beyond personal relationships—if we saw entire families, communities, or all of humanity as part of the same team? Imagine how we'd treat each other.

It has long been declared that the nature of life is based on survival of the fittest—that we all must constantly compete to survive. And maybe in some ways this is true. But what if there were another truth, something that is even more powerful than competition? What if cooperation is our true natural state?

I have experienced the power of cooperation. I know how much better life feels when I choose to work *with* rather than *against* the people in my world. When I am willing to find ways to communicate, to release blame and criticism, to connect with the people I share this life with, I open myself to more joy and ease.

When I slip into the mind-set of competing with my husband for who has more free time, or who has contributed more to our family, or who has initiated more acts of kindness, I feel detached, separate, and pretty horrible. This is the underlying effect of competition; we envision ourselves as separate. We lose touch with our interconnectedness, our wholeness, our oneness.

I notice this with my children. When my girls are expressing angst toward one another, I recognize that their antagonistic behavior is not so much about being mean or hateful, but rather a request for attention. They each want to know that they matter, that they are a valuable part of their family, that they are connected with the people upon whom they rely for nurturing.

It seems to me that perhaps competitive nature is not so much the natural state of being, but rather a result of feeling disconnected from the security and certainty of being part of something greater than ourselves. I think, in fact, that cooperation is our true nature. We must work together to survive, to thrive, to evolve. Sometimes a competitive attitude can be useful, but for our collective growth and happiness, we must learn to embrace a new truth: we are one.

SEPTEMBER 22

Challenge

In conversations today, give up the need to be right and to prove others wrong.

For Reflection

With whom do you frequently feel the need to prove that you're right and they're wrong?

What topics of conversation are most likely to lead to this type of exchange?

How could you respond differently to set a tone of respect and acceptance, and stop making it a competition?

How Did It Go?

How did it change your interactions to stop defending your point of view?

SEPTEMBER 23

Challenge

Whenever you find yourself keeping score today, thinking you've done or given more than someone else, stop and recognize something the other person has done—and (bonus!) thank them.

For Reflection

In which relationship have you been keeping score?

Are there any little things you've received from this person that you may have overlooked because you've been focused on what you think you're not getting?

If you weren't tracking every little thing, would you consider this to be a healthy, balanced relationship? If not, what is the bigger issue that needs to be addressed?

How Did It Go?

How successful were you at not keeping score today? Did you feel differently about your relationships as a result?

SEPTEMBER 24

Challenge

Thank someone who helped you achieve a goal recently in order to communicate your gratitude, and to remind both them and yourself that we are all interconnected, and we can all help and support each other.

For Reflection

How did this person help you reach your goal?

What difficulties might you have encountered had you not received their support?

How did achieving this goal make a meaningful difference in your life?

How Did It Go?

Did the other person seem touched or surprised to realize they helped you in this way?

SEPTEMBER 25

Challenge

Help someone else shine today to practice lifting others up without feeling threatened or tempted to compete.

Brainstorm: *For example, ask a friend to talk about her recent promotion or her new passion project while out with a group of friends, or, during a meeting, ask a coworker to elaborate on the great idea he shared over lunch.*

For Reflection

Do you already do this regularly? If not, why? What thoughts or fears prevent you from doing this?

Has anyone ever done this for you? If so, what did you most appreciate, and why?

How might your relationships improve if you felt you were all "sharing the stage," and no one had to feel less worthy, accomplished, or important than anyone else?

How Did It Go?

Who did you help shine today? Did it feel good to shine a spotlight on someone else in this way, and do you think they appreciated this?

SEPTEMBER 26

Challenge

Write below what you think healthy competition and unhealthy competition look like, and what you can do or tell yourself when you're tempted to compete in an unhealthy way. Utilize this knowledge today if you catch yourself competing in a way that will be detrimental to you, your loved ones, or your relationships.

Healthy Competition:

Unhealthy Competition:

What you can do to help yourself when you start competing in an unhealthy way:

How Did It Go?

Was this exercise helpful to you? Were you tempted to compete in an unhealthy way today?

SEPTEMBER 27

Challenge

Create a win/win situation with someone today instead of trying to win at someone else's expense.

Brainstorm: *Instead of demanding that your roommate do the dishes so you can relax, offer to wash if she dries so you can finish more quickly and both have more time to relax; instead of asking your spouse to cancel his plans for the evening so he can watch the kids and you can go out, ask if he'll consider pushing his plans back an hour so you can have a little time to yourself before he heads out.*

For Reflection

Is this something you already do regularly, or are you more likely to create win/lose situations, where one person gets what they want and the other doesn't?

If you chose the latter, why do you think you do this, and how does it affect your relationships?

How does it affect your feelings toward others when they try to create win/win situations instead of striving to "win" at your expense?

How Did It Go?

What win/win situation did you create, and how did the other person respond?

SEPTEMBER 28

Challenge

Make eye contact and smile at a homeless person today to let them know (and to remind yourself) that they are not beneath you.

For Reflection

Have you ever looked down on a homeless person—and if so, why?

How have you responded to them as a result of this?

How would you hope others would see and treat you if you were down on your luck someday?

How Did It Go?

What feelings came up when you did this? How did the homeless person respond to your acknowledgment?

SEPTEMBER 29

Challenge

Identify one person you often compare unfavorably to someone in your past. Now identify one reason you're grateful for this relationship as it is, and share this with them.

Brainstorm: *It might be a frugal boyfriend you compare to a generous ex, or an introverted friend you compare to a former friend who was the life of the party.*

For Reflection

What do you feel is lacking in this relationship that wasn't lacking in your former one?

How does it negatively impact the relationship to hold this person to an unfair standard?

How does this block you from recognizing and appreciating what's good about this unique relationship?

How Did It Go?

What did you thank this person for, and how did they respond? Did this help you let go of the past and appreciate what you have in the present?

SEPTEMBER 30

Challenge

Identify one way you can work in cooperation with a competitor or someone who is striving toward a similar goal. Contact this person today to propose helping and supporting each other in this way.

For Reflection

Have you ever worked together with someone you considered a competitor to further your mutual goals?

How were you stronger as a team supporting each other than individuals competing with each other?

If you knew someone else's success and happiness wouldn't in any way detract from your own, how would you feel about helping them reach their goals?

How Did It Go?

Who did you choose to work with today, and how? Did it change your feelings about this person to join forces in this way?

MONTHLY REVIEW

- Which challenges were the most helpful for you, and why?
- Which challenges were the most difficult for you, and why?
- What did you learn about yourself through the process of completing these challenges? Did you form any new insights about releasing comparisons and competition?
- What did you learn about the people in your life?
- Did these challenges strengthen your relationships, and how?
- Did you identify any areas for improvement and growth?
- Head over to http://tinybuddha.com/love-forums to share your experiences with other readers!

OCTOBER

Support and Encouragement

Reflections from CLAIRE DE BOER

When my best friend lost her five-year-old daughter to meningitis last Christmas, I wanted to squeeze that pain right out of her with my love. Instead, I held back, watching for the lights to go on in the house, as the family of four returned home from the hospital as a family of three.

For two days I stayed away because I didn't know what to say. I wanted to give her space and knew that her phone would be ringing constantly, and I used these as excuses to avoid facing the unthinkable—holding a friend facing the one tragedy no parent should ever have to experience. On day three I knocked on her door. I couldn't stay away any longer. We held each other close on her doorstep, her crying in my arms, me looking down at the floor where sparkly pink shoes and a Disney backpack lay strewn in the doorway. Emily's last day in kindergarten.

The house was so full of this child—pajamas on the couch, toys she had played with only days earlier, her writing on the chalkboard in the kitchen. And yet this blue-eyed girl with her infectious smile and the honey-colored knots that couldn't be brushed would never play in that room again. If my heart ached this much, how unbearable must it have been for my friend?

We sat among unopened gifts, vases of flowers, and Tupperware containers of food prepared by neighbors. I wanted to say something beyond "I'm sorry"—something profound that would ease her pain, but no words would come. It seemed like there couldn't possibly be anything big enough for me to say. So I let her tell me. About the fever and the sickness, how she thought it was the flu. And then the rush to the hospital, the swarm of doctors, and the race to intensive care. How she held her baby all night, even after she was gone.

And still I had no words. What do we say when someone experiences a loss so tragic? What can possibly make a difference? So I said, "I'm sorry," pulled my friend's head into my shoulder, and listened.

I have learned in the months since that little girl passed away that the pain never dies, and there are no words that can ever lessen the agony a parent endures. To know this, to know that every day is torture and months and years may pass but the pain never leaves, this is how we support someone through grief.

The meals stopped within a few weeks, as did the flowers and cards. Life went on. That's the hardest part, I noticed, continuing with life when a loved one has gone. There are the anniversaries—the sixth birthday for the girl who would always be five, the start of a new school year for the girl who would always be in kindergarten, and *that* day—the anniversary of her death.

And in that gap, that void where grief and loneliness collide, is where I found my new place as her friend. In sitting by her side and letting her talk. In standing in Emily's closet, watching my friend run her fingers through clothes that would never be worn. In nighttime phone conversations recalling memories of camping trips and the day Emily learned to ride a bike. In remaining by her side and listening.

OCTOBER 1

Challenge

Tell someone who recently experienced a great hardship or tragedy, "I'm here for you if you ever want to talk—and I'm here for you if you don't."

For Reflection

Can you think of a time when you needed someone to be there for you, without saying anything specific?

Was anyone able to offer you this kind of nonverbal support? If so, how did it benefit you to be in their presence without needing to talk?

Have you done this for someone else before? If so, did it seem to help?

How Did It Go?

Who did you offer your support, and did they seem to appreciate this?

OCTOBER 2

Challenge

Offer practical support to someone who is overwhelmed, stressed, or struggling with some type of hardship.

Brainstorm: *Take a meal to a friend who's recently lost a loved one, offer to pick up a loved one's prescription, or offer to research therapists for a depressed friend.*

For Reflection

Has anyone ever offered you this kind of practical support when you were going through a tough time? If so, how was this helpful to you?

Would it have occurred to you to ask someone for this kind of help? Why or why not?

What type of practical support would be most helpful for your loved one, and why?

How Did It Go?

What did you do or offer to do, and how do you think this made a difference in your loved one's life?

OCTOBER 3

Challenge

Reach out to a loved one who recently experienced a failure or setback to encourage them to keep going.

For Reflection

How has this setback affected this person's self-confidence?

What do you think they could accomplish if they didn't take this setback to heart?

What can you do or say to encourage them to keep going, in spite of this experience?

How Did It Go?

What did you say? Did your encouragement seem to make a difference?

OCTOBER 4

Challenge

Identify one supportive phrase you wish you had heard more growing up. Every time you pass by a mirror today, look at yourself and say this.

For Reflection

Why do you wish you had heard this phrase more growing up?

How did not hearing this affect your belief in yourself?

How might your life change if you fully internalized this?

How Did It Go?

How did you feel when you said this to yourself, and did you find this encouraging?

OCTOBER 5

Challenge

Help a loved one get new clients by promoting their business or service with a mass e-mail or social media update.

For Reflection

How does this business enable your loved one to live a fulfilling, purpose-driven life?

What makes their business or service unique or worthwhile?

How might you make a difference in their life by sharing this with your network?

How Did It Go?

What did you write, and did anyone comment on this? Do you think this helped generate new leads for your loved one?

OCTOBER 6

Challenge

Share an encouraging YouTube video with a friend who could benefit from a virtual pep talk.

Brainstorm: *Nick Vujicic, born with no arms and legs, offers an inspiring message about getting back up after you fall (http://tinybuddha.com/get-up) and SoulPancake's Kid President shares a message of encouragement for anyone who needs a kick in the right direction (http://tinybuddha.com/kid-president-pep-talk).*

For Reflection

What do you believe is the root of your friend's struggle?

What do you wish they realized about themselves and their potential?

What do you hope this video inspires them to do?

How Did It Go?

What video did you share, and did your friend find it encouraging?

OCTOBER 7

Challenge

Offer to buy lunch for a friend who is struggling financially. If *you* are struggling financially, offer to buy them a coffee or soda instead.

For Reflection

Why has this person been struggling financially, and how has this affected their mood, their relationships, and their life in general?

What could you afford to give, and how can you offer it in a way that won't make them feel worse about themselves?

How Did It Go?

What did you offer to do? Did your friend accept?

After planning the next three months of my life in my head, trying to focus on my breath, and recounting the plans for tomorrow, I decided my battle with insomnia was going to win. I got up, careful not to wake my husband, and decided to start reading. Nestling into the lines of my latest library book well after midnight, my phone began to beep.

I thought to myself, *Who else could be awake at this hour?* It was my twin sister all the way across the country, struggling with insomnia herself. Ready to share my latest updates with her, something encouraged me to ask how she was doing and why she was still awake. It was in the stillness of the late evening that I slowed down to think of someone other than myself. I wondered, if the sun was brightly shining and I was carrying on with my own busyness, would I have answered her text message? If I were rushing through the day, would I have noticed her hint of sadness?

She recounted the daily stressors and recent disagreement with a friend. In her written words, I sensed an echo of loneliness, a tinge of yearning for connection. So often in the busyness of our own self-absorbed lives we fail to notice when others are in need of connection. If we are in need, can't we recognize that others are too? So many of us feel alone in our day-to-day trials, but as I remember learning as a young girl, when we focus our love on others, it betters our own hearts too.

As my sister and I completed our novel-length texts back and forth, she said she appreciated the words we shared and I saw our conversation as an illustration of her trust in me. We may not all have those two o'clock in the morning bonding opportunities with our siblings as the rest of the world dreams, but we all have twenty-four hours to seek out a wounded soul in need of our light.

I moved abroad to support my husband's career and offer new possibilities to my children. After the dust settled, I felt stuck. Lonely. Helpless. Desperate. What was I going to do with my life? Was this the end of my professional career? I used to earn more than my partner. Now I had become like a child, relying on him for money, housing, health care, and a visa.

Craving connections but not knowing where to find meaningful relationships, I skimmed the Internet. I started to read about grief and loss, and I understood why I felt so depressed. I also started following bloggers who taught me to take one step at a time. They said I mattered. They said they cared. I believed them. Then I started my own blog and wrote articles about the psychological challenges I met: grief, loss of identity, financial dependence, raising multilingual children in multicultural settings.

In the meantime, thousands of miles away, Carla was a stay-at-home mom living in the Netherlands. She had been uprooted several times: four countries in seven years.

She was waking anxious each morning. Almost in a panic. She was exhausted with trying to make new connections, and she still didn't understand the language. Once, at her son's international school, she got so intimidated that she couldn't even enter the meeting room where parents had been invited for an informal breakfast.

One day, Carla found my blog and sent me an e-mail. I answered and we started a conversation. I didn't do anything magical; I just listened. I told her that she mattered to me and that I cared. And she believed me. Little by little, she got more confident. She eventually worked up the courage to ask another mom for coffee. A few days later, she pushed open the door and joined the parents' meeting at school. She had overcome her fear of rejection. She wasn't paralyzed anymore.

Last week, she wrote to me: she's organizing a coffee with eleven moms at her home! She's now connecting other people with each other. And so we keep the chain of support alive.

OCTOBER 8

Challenge

When you find yourself getting caught up in your head, thinking only about yourself and everything you have to do, stop and ask someone else how they're doing.

For Reflection

Do you ever get so busy that you forget to consider the people around you?

Do you ever get frustrated when other people seem too busy to consider you?

Has anyone ever made time for you when you knew they were busy, and how did this affect you?

How Did It Go?

Who did you ask this question, and how did they respond? Did shifting your focus outside yourself affect you in a positive way?

OCTOBER 9

Challenge

Write something supportive or encouraging on a blog post, forum post, or social media update.

Brainstorm: *You could comment on someone's poem, photograph, or artwork "You're so talented—I should get your autograph now before you're famous!" Or you could respond to a forum posting seeking advice at http://tinybuddha.com/forums.*

For Reflection

Has anyone ever made a huge difference in your life by offering support or encouragement online?

What did they write, and how and why was this helpful to you?

Who in your life would benefit the most from a little support or encouragement?

How Did It Go?

What did you write, and do you think it helped?

OCTOBER 10

Challenge

Send an uplifting card or e-card to someone who could use it.

Tip: *Google "free e-cards" and you'll find tons of options.*

For Reflection

Who in your life could use a little uplifting, and why? What has this person been going through, and how do you imagine they've felt as a result?

Have you ever struggled with anything similar? If so, what do you wish someone said (or wrote) to you then?

Would you prefer a handwritten card or an e-card from someone? Why would you prefer this over the other?

How Did It Go?

Did you send a handwritten card or an e-card? If it was an e-card, did you receive a response?

OCTOBER 11

Challenge

Ask someone how they're doing with their progress toward one of their goals, and if there's anything you can do to help.

For Reflection

Why is this particular goal important to your loved one? How will achieving it change their life for the better?

How have they struggled in working toward this goal?

How could you use your skills and strengths to help?

How Did It Go?

How did this person respond? Did they decide to take you up on your offer?

OCTOBER 12

Challenge

Write down three ways you've made personal or professional progress recently. Read this several times throughout the day to encourage yourself to keep working toward your goals.

Ways You've Made Progress:

1.

2.

3.

How Did It Go?

Did focusing on your progress encourage you to keep going?

OCTOBER 13

Challenge

Google a cause that interests you, and identify one small (or large) way that you could offer your support.

For Reflection

What type of cause would be most personally meaningful for you, and why?

What's prevented you from supporting this cause in the past? If this is still an obstacle now, what would help you overcome this?

In what way would you most enjoy supporting this cause? By volunteering in person? By lending your skills from home? By making a financial donation?

How Did It Go?

What cause did you google, and how did you choose to support it?

OCTOBER 14

Challenge

Find an online or offline support group that might be helpful to a friend. Then e-mail them the link with a note explaining how this could help them reach their goal or better deal with their current challenge.

For Reflection

Have you ever utilized a support group to help you overcome a challenge or reach a goal?

How did it help you to connect with others who were going through the same thing?

Who in your life could most benefit from this same support?

How Did It Go?

What group did you find, and did your friend seem open to the idea of joining?

My significant other and I met under messy circumstances. Both just weeks out of intense breakups and deeply embroiled in "processing" our respective experiences, I had a laundry list of emotional baggage to shed, patterns to break, and new nonnegotiable standards for anything and anyone I'd allow into my intimate space.

I saw myself as an evolved and conscious woman doing the work to grow. I journaled, meditated, and prayed. And as I learned, dove deeper, and sailed higher, I held fiercely to my partner's hand. I wanted to do this together. I begged him: join me. Rise. Dig. Excavate your stagnant places. It's the only way forward. I believed it. And I think, to a certain end, so did he.

Then our relationship's encouragement, collaborative growth, and tough love turned to jagged criticism. Instead of holding each other in our struggles, we sat on opposing sides of some false fence. I saw only his flaws and I believed I needed him to fix them. I saw his potential. He was brilliant, deeply spiritual, an intuitive outdoorsman, and an incredible teacher. He had promise, and gifts to bring to the world. I wanted him to reach for his potential—without fear. And when he didn't, when he paused to rest, when he stumbled, I saw failure. I saw an unwillingness to try. I saw a man gripped by fear, clinging to safety. I used those words. Why couldn't he work as hard as me?

It's easy to say this now. To see where my ardent desires for his evolution—to step into his highest self—so quickly became toxic. How it clouded my vision of who he was, in the moment, without the changes I thought necessary. Wrapped up in my own work, I transposed my journey onto his.

All I saw was his shining potential, his shadowed present, and the moments when he wasn't up to the challenge. I ignored the brilliant light already standing in front of me, showing up in his wholeness, wounds and all. So he learned to try and hide these flaws, for fear that I would criticize the most tender parts.

His imperfections became my teachers. And as I crumbled, defeated in my epic pursuit of New Age Girlfriend Perfection, he taught me what it is to hold someone you love to their highest potential, with grace, love, and honor.

If you find yourself doing more criticizing and pushing than supporting and encouraging, spend more time celebrating the positive elements of how far your partner has already come—and then encourage them to keep going, because you see such beautiful potential and brightness within. Remember that you're not his life coach. You're not her personal trainer. You're not their mom. Position yourself on the same team—encouraging, supporting, celebrating, yes. Demanding? No. That creates a power dynamic that eventually becomes toxic and corrodes the integrity of your relationship.

When you find yourself becoming the teacher, check your motivations and rephrase. How can you encourage with tender and gracious love? You have this one role in your partner's evolution: to hold the space, to fill it with love and safety, and, simultaneously, the encouragement to expand. Your love will become their freedom. Freedom to be exactly where they are on the path and to take the journey that is right at that moment and in that time. Freedom to fall. To screw up. And to try again, with unflinching faith in their own potential. And that freedom, ultimately, is the only path to the highest self.

OCTOBER 15

Challenge

Identify an area where a friend or your significant other has made tremendous growth, and let them know how and why this has inspired you.

For Reflection

How has this person grown, and why do you think these changes may have been difficult to make?

Have you learned anything in watching this person grow that will help you improve yourself or your life?

What do you think this person might appreciate about knowing how they've inspired you?

How Did It Go?

How did your friend respond to your observation? Do you think this encouraged them to continue with the good progress they've been making?

OCTOBER 16

Challenge

Tell someone in your life about the potential you see in them, personally or professionally.

For Reflection

Who in your life struggles to recognize their potential for happiness, passion, purpose, or fulfillment?

What do you see in them that you wish they saw as well?

What do you believe they could do if only they believed in themselves?

How Did It Go?

What did you share? Did the person seem open to seeing themselves in the way you see them?

OCTOBER 17

Challenge

Offer someone something tangible or intangible that may support their growth or help them reach one of their goals.

Brainstorm: *Lend a friend your car to drive to an interview or your yoga mat so she can try a class, or give your time by proofreading your boyfriend's résumé or listening to your mother's speech for an upcoming event.*

For Reflection

Has anyone ever done something like this for you? If so, how did this assistance affect your morale and motivation?

Who in your life could most benefit from this same support right now, and why?

What do you feel most comfortable giving, and how do you think this might help them?

How Did It Go?

What did you offer, and how did the other person respond? Do you think your help made a big difference?

OCTOBER 18

Challenge

Tell someone one reason you're proud of yourself, both to vocally offer yourself encouragement and to model for that person what this looks like.

For Reflection

What's something you've done, felt, thought, attempted, or changed that you feel proud of, and why?

How might it benefit someone else to share this?

Do you usually share with other people when you feel proud of yourself—and if not, why?

How Did It Go?

What did you share? How did you feel after sharing this, and do you think it was helpful to the other person?

OCTOBER 19

Challenge

Write below your greatest accomplishment ever (even if it isn't recent), one person whose support was instrumental in achieving that goal, and how this made a difference in your life. Get in touch with that person today, even if through a brief e-mail, to share what their support meant to you.

Your greatest accomplishment:

Whose support was instrumental in achieving your goal:

How this made a difference in your life:

How Did It Go?

Was the other person surprised to learn just how much they've impacted your life?

OCTOBER 20

Challenge

Write the words *You did a great job on this!* on a sticky note, and leave it near something someone did well.

Brainstorm: *You could leave this on your child's school project before going to sleep, near the garage your husband just cleaned out, or near your girlfriend's painting.*

For Reflection

When was the last time someone told you that you did a great job on something?

How did you feel about yourself and your work as a result?

Do you regularly give out this kind of praise? If not, why?

How Did It Go?

Who did you praise, and for what? How do you think this affected them?

OCTOBER 21

Challenge

Any time you're tempted to nag someone today, offer a few words of praise or encouragement instead.

For Reflection

Who in your life do you often nag, and why do you think you do this?

How do they respond to this, and how does it affect your relationship?

What would you need to let go of to be less demanding and more encouraging?

How Did It Go?

Were you tempted to nag people today? If so, how did you encourage them instead, and how did this affect your interactions?

I left my marriage in a way that didn't allow for an amicable separation, or an easy transition as we redefined our roles and responsibilities as coparents. After being left with a Dear John letter, most men would have held a heavy bitterness to the grave. And don't get me started on the emotional junk that I had stored up from our twelve-year relationship (perceived or real). Somehow we transformed the dysfunctional marriage into damn good parenting, even if we didn't live together.

I've tried to nail down the "why" and the "how" of our relationship. How did we survive the emotional roller-coaster loop-de-loops with grace, while others turned green and lost their lunch? Was it sheer *luck* that kept the drama of our separation and marriage out of our new divorced (now blended) family?

One day, as I was reading my ex's reply to the banal e-mail chain about first-grader schedules and piano lessons, it hit me! He wrote: "I find myself appreciating us lately. Parenting doesn't get easier just because our child learns better communication . . . it's actually the opposite. And I applaud us. It's hard sometimes, but I love us."

In years past, I would have waited for the other shoe to drop. I would have looked for the "catch" in his statement. But today, I knew to the core that it was authentic and it was loving and it was encouragement. Encouragement! *That* was our secret weapon against bitterness. In one grand flash I remembered five years' worth of texts and awkward social moments ending with: "This is hard, but I'm proud of us." Or "You are a great dad." Or "She is lucky to have you as a mom."

Yes, we have a coparenting plan. Yes, we have boundaries. But the consistent giving of mustard-seed-sized encouragement has made all the difference.

My younger brother, Justin, and I took sibling rivalry to the limit when we were younger. We would fight about anything and everything. As we aged, the competition didn't fully go away, but our relationship grew into a friendship built on love and support. I would spend long nights with him, helping him with his schoolwork. He would bring me crumpled binder paper with a half-finished portion of his latest writing assignment, written in barely legible handwriting. He had some of the worst handwriting ever, probably because his hand was too big for the pencil.

And so it would go, I would support and encourage him, and in turn he would support and encourage me. When I decided to move with my now fiancé to Los Angeles to start a life together and to pursue my dreams, it was my brother who loaded our furniture, drove the U-Haul, and helped move us in.

My fiancé and I moved with very little money, and our relationship was young and had not yet been tested. Since we could barely support ourselves, we didn't devote much money to date nights. Then, in the mail one day, arrived an envelope. Inside was a $100 gift card to Benihana's, one of our favorite restaurants, and a note, written on a miniature piece of binder paper, with very familiar crooked letters, reading:

> Dear Ehren, I hope you are having success in LA, and that all of your dreams are coming true. Well, be safe and hopefully you guys can have a couple of dates on me. Love, Justin

My brother has since passed away, but his loving gesture still stirs inside me, and always will. Even though I thanked him at the time, he may have never known how much his gift aided my now strong relationship, and how much a crumpled piece of paper has meant to me. I carry it to this day, as a symbol of his support and our bond, and as a reminder to show others the same love he showed me.

OCTOBER 22

Challenge

Encourage someone to do something you know they want to do, and tell them you believe in them.

For Reflection

Who in your life has wanted to do something but has hesitated due to fear or doubt?

Why do you believe they can and should push themselves to do this? How will their life change for the better if they give it a go?

What's something you could say to help them overcome their fear or resistance?

How Did It Go?

What did you encourage this person to do, and were they open to this suggestion?

OCTOBER 23

Challenge

Commend one of your coworkers to your/their boss to support their professional growth.

For Reflection

Which one of your coworkers has done an exceptional job lately? How have they gone above and beyond?

How might it benefit your coworker to share this with their supervisor?

Do you feel comfortable doing this? If not, why, and how can you overcome this?

How Did It Go?

What did you share, and how did their supervisor respond? How do you think you made a difference in your coworker's life?

OCTOBER 24

Challenge

Write a recommendation for someone on LinkedIn or offer to write a testimonial for their product or service.

For Reflection

Has anyone ever done something like this for you? If so, what did you appreciate about this?

Who do you know that is looking for work or is unsatisfied with their current job, and what can you emphasize in your recommendation to increase their odds of catching an employer's eye?

How Did It Go?

What did you write in your recommendation? Was this person excited to see this?

OCTOBER 25

Challenge

Reinforce someone's skills or strengths by telling them:
"You're one of the best ____________ I know."

For Reflection

Who in your life excels at their job or impresses you with their passion and talent outside of work?

Why do you believe they are amazing at what they do?

How and why does this impress or inspire you?

How Did It Go?

Who did you offer this praise, and how did they respond? Did they seem surprised to realize you hold them in such high regard?

OCTOBER 26

Challenge

Share an image with an encouraging quote on one of your social media pages. If you don't have any social media pages, e-mail one of these images to a friend who might appreciate it.

Brainstorm: *You can find some great options in the photo album here: http://facebook.com/tinybuddha. You can also do a Google image search for your favorite encouraging quote.*

For Reflection

Has an image like this ever offered you a much-needed boost in the middle of a busy, stressful, or overwhelming day?

Which quote do you find most encouraging, and why?

How Did It Go?

What quote did you choose, and did anyone comment on it?

OCTOBER 27

Challenge

Keep an eye out for someone who seems to go above and beyond in their job, and let them know you noticed and you admire them for it.

Brainstorm: *This could be a coworker, or it could be someone you see throughout your day, like a friendly postal worker or an attentive sales associate.*

For Reflection

Do you usually reserve compliments like this for people you know?

Have you ever complimented a stranger on how they did their job before? If yes, how did the person respond to this, and how do you think it affected their day?

What prevents you from noticing and commenting on the good work people around you do?

How Did It Go?

Whose work did you observe today, and what did you say to acknowledge it? How did they respond?

OCTOBER 28

Challenge

Tell a street artist, musician, or performer that they're talented and you think they have a great future ahead of them.

For Reflection

Have you ever passed by a street artist, musician, or performer that you believed to be incredibly talented?

Did you stop to offer a donation or words of praise?

If yes, how do you believe this affected them—and if no, what prevented you from doing this?

How Did It Go?

Who did you praise, and why? How did they receive your words of encouragement?

OCTOBER 29

Challenge

Encourage a busy friend to step away from their work for a while and do something relaxing or enjoyable. (Bonus: join in, if you feel like it!)

Brainstorm: *Hike or go bike riding, access your inner child and hop on some swings in the park, or walk down the street for a hot chocolate or ice cream (depending on the weather where you live).*

For Reflection

Has anyone ever offered you a reminder like this when you were tempted to push yourself too hard?

Did you take this advice, and if so, how did it affect your mood? Did it also affect your productivity?

What other benefits of relaxing can you share to help convince your friend to take a break?

How Did It Go?

Did your friend take your advice? Did you join? How do you think this made a difference in their day, and how did it make a difference in yours?

OCTOBER 30

Challenge

Think about an area of your life where you try your hardest but sometimes feel you're falling short. Recall all the critical things you've said to yourself, and think about what you'd tell a friend if you knew they were being hard on themselves in this way. Now complete the writing prompt below so you'll have this for encouragement whenever you need a reminder that you're doing the best you can.

You may not always believe it, but you're doing an amazing job at . . .

How Did It Go?

Did you form any helpful new insights or write anything that surprised you? How did you feel after completing this exercise?

OCTOBER 31

Challenge

Identify a friend who could benefit from learning one of your skills, and offer to teach it to them (or teach them enough about it to get them started).

For Reflection

Who in your life could benefit from learning one of your skills, whether it's something you use at work or something you use in your free time?

How would it improve their life if they learned this skill?

What could you share with them to help them get started?

How Did It Go?

Who did you offer this help, and did they accept it? How did you feel knowing you were leveraging your strengths to make a positive difference in someone's life?

MONTHLY REVIEW

- Which challenges were the most helpful for you, and why?
- Which challenges were the most difficult for you, and why?
- What did you learn about yourself through the process of completing these challenges? Did you form any new insights about giving support and encouragement?
- What did you learn about the people in your life?
- Did these challenges strengthen your relationships, and how?
- Did you identify any areas for improvement and growth?
- Head over to http://tinybuddha.com/love-forums to share your experiences with other readers!

NOVEMBER

Admiration and Appreciation

Reflections from **ELLEN BARD**

Over six hundred people attended my dad's funeral. That day, I was able to see the impact he'd made on hundreds of people's lives in the condolences book, the online tributes left on the local radio station's website where he was the religious presenter, and in the hundreds of letters and cards sent to my mom, sister, and me.

The tributes told stories of wisdom, faith, support, warmth, generosity, and, most of all, humor. They made me cry and laugh at the same time. In the bitter first stages of grief, I was grateful to each and every loving person who took the time to write and share their thoughts and feelings about how Dad had supported or helped them.

But I wondered, how often had these same individuals taken the opportunity to let my father know about their appreciation or admiration for him? He had a huge capacity for love, and was clearly loved in return, but did he know the impact and influence he had had on these diverse lives?

This experience reminded me to tell the people who have made an impact on me, taught me something, or been a role model that I'm grateful. I've learned to say thank you for little kindnesses, laughter, compassion, lessons, and love. And in turn, perhaps even harder, I learned to acknowledge others when they say thank you to me—to recognize and accept their thanks.

Creating these tiny reciprocal and positive "strokes" (as Transactional Analysis calls such pieces of recognition from one person to another) are what makes for healthy communication and living. We hunger for this kind of attention, which in turn builds our self-image and connects us with others. I learned the importance of these "strokes." And the experience taught me to share them with the individual themselves too, before death makes it impossible. Whose strokes are you discounting or ignoring? Who do you need to "stroke" today?

Reflections from WILFRIED LEHMKUHLER

I was not an easy son. I fought my parents, especially my dad, every opportunity I had. In my midtwenties I finally grew up, started my first business, and got married. After years of fighting, it was not easy to rebuild the relationship with my father. But despite struggling with my stubbornness, we slowly made progress.

The day after my wedding, my dad drove my wife and me to the airport to start our honeymoon. As he dropped us off, my dad and I hugged and he said, "When you guys come back, we will talk."

Three days later I received a phone call from my mother. My dad had died during a massive heart attack. I got a sick feeling in my stomach, as though someone pulled the rug from under my feet and I was falling at the speed of light. I would never see my dad again—I was not ready for this! After the call, I screamed and wailed for hours. The pain was overwhelming. Suddenly, I realized that I did not have a chance to tell him how much I loved him, how much I regret being difficult for so many years, and how disappointed I was that I did not have a chance to resolve this with him.

It took me years before I could forgive myself for what happened, but I was eventually able to open myself up for a valuable life lesson: the lesson of appreciation. Nowadays, I'm much more aware about leaving things unresolved with people close to me. Life is too short and the days given to us are far too precious.

Let's not waste energy on stubbornness, but work out our disagreements. To live with regret is horrible; don't let this happen to you. Make an effort not to part in anger or bitterness; instead, appreciate the people in your life while you can.

NOVEMBER 1

Challenge

Imagine you needed to write a eulogy for your best friend, and identify at least one positive thing you'd say about that person. Share that praise with them today instead of waiting until they're not here to hear it.

For Reflection

Which of your friend's strengths or traits do you find most admirable?

How has your friend made a positive difference in your life?

Is there anything you'd say that you've never told them before—and why haven't you done this?

How Did It Go?

How did your friend respond? Were they surprised you felt this way?

NOVEMBER 2

Challenge

Text or e-mail someone: "I don't think I ever thanked you for . . ." (Or, if you feel inclined, say it face-to-face.)

Brainstorm: *This could be something your parents did for you when you were younger, how your friend listened when you needed to talk recently, or how your spouse cooked your favorite meal last week.*

For Reflection

Has anyone done this for you recently? If so, what touched you most about this?

Do you usually express appreciation right away? If times goes by, are you less likely to do it? Why or why not?

Has anyone done anything little for you recently that had a bigger impact than they likely know?

How Did It Go?

Who did you thank, and for what? Did they seem touched that you did this?

NOVEMBER 3

Challenge

Make a toast to someone—alcohol not required—
recognizing something they did well recently
or something you admire about them.

Brainstorm: *You could toast a coworker's promotion over lunch, your significant other's progress toward a goal over dinner, or your friend's general awesomeness at happy hour.*

For Reflection

Has anyone you're planning to see today accomplished anything you find impressive or inspiring?

Has anyone you're planning to see today done something little worth recognizing—something that's actually a lot bigger than it seems?

What would you most appreciate hearing if someone were to make a toast to you?

How Did It Go?

Who did you toast, and why? How did they respond?

NOVEMBER 4

Challenge

Thank someone today for an intangible gift—for example, their time, attention, understanding, or support.

For Reflection

Who in your life has given you something intangible but invaluable lately?

Do you think they realize just how helpful this was to you?

How did this gift make a difference in your day, or your life?

How Did It Go?

What did you say, and how did the other person respond? Did they seem to appreciate that you recognized the value of this gift?

NOVEMBER 5

Challenge

E-mail yourself a note of appreciation—for anything. Save it to read whenever you need a reminder of how amazing you are.

For Reflection

Have you done anything lately that you feel proud of?

How do you think you make a positive difference in the world?

Is there anything you wish others would recognize and appreciate about you?

How Did It Go?

Did you read the e-mail at any point today? If so, how did that affect your state of mind and your day?

NOVEMBER 6

Challenge

Take a picture of yourself wearing or using a gift someone gave you, and text or e-mail it to them with a note of appreciation.

For Reflection

Can you think of any recent birthday or holiday gifts that you've appreciated and used a lot?

Why have you enjoyed and appreciated this gift?

How Did It Go?

What gift did you choose, and what did you write in the text or e-mail? How did the other person respond?

NOVEMBER 7

Challenge

Make a list of traits you find admirable, and look for people who demonstrate these traits throughout your day so you can voice your admiration.

Brainstorm: *If you choose confidence, you could praise a coworker for speaking up in a meeting; if you choose compassion, you could praise a friend who sticks up for someone else.*

Traits you find admirable and why:

How Did It Go?

Who did you acknowledge today? Did you compliment more people than you usually do?

Reflections from GIGI GRIFFIS

When I was seventeen years old, I decided to make a change. Every time I had a kind thought about someone, I was going to tell them. And anytime I heard a compliment about someone who wasn't in the room, I would let them know. I wasn't in the habit of doling out compliments. And, yet, when I got a random compliment, it changed the shape of my entire day, sometimes my entire week. So I decided to change.

If I loved someone's outfit in the grocery store, I said so. When my sister did something brave, I told her. When I felt a rush of affection for my best friend, I voiced it. And when someone called a colleague brilliant, I shot them a note.

It sounds like a pretty simple change to make, but even simple changes can be hard because so much of what we do is habit. If we've been keeping our thoughts to ourselves for twenty or thirty years, it can be tough to start speaking up. But when you do make a commitment to make a small change like that, it can have a massive ripple effect. It can change your relationships. It can change your perspective. It can change the course of a life. And boy, did it for me.

The first time I complimented a stranger, he fell in love with me. Other times I earned smiles, thoughtful pauses, and quiet, sincere thank-yous. But the most powerful change I saw was the ripple effect that my decision had on those around me, and in particular, on two girls that I met on a trip to Costa Rica later that year. It was a volunteer trip for teenagers and I was what they called a MAG Leader—a sort of camp counselor who roomed with five girls and took responsibility for their well-being.

Two of the five girls did not get along. They barely spoke, and when they did, it was to antagonize the other. One girl made physical threats. Both did a lot of talking behind each other's back—until I introduced my compliment commitment to the group.

I sat the girls in a circle and handed out index cards. Each index card had one of our names written on the front. And I told the girls that we were going to take a few minutes to pass around these cards.

On each card, they should write one thing they really admired about the person whose name was on the card. One sincere compliment. Afterward, each girl got the card with her name on it. At the end of the few minutes we spent with these index cards, the two teenaged enemies were shocked to discover that the other person had something really insightful to put on their card. One girl commented on the strength and confidence of the other. The second girl admired the poise of the first.

Suddenly, these girls respected each other. Suddenly, they each had something positive to say about the other. They never became best friends. But the bad-mouthing and the threats and the antagonism melted away. A grudging respect, and even courtesy, took their place. This is when I really understood the power of compliments. The power of saying the kind things we think.

It doesn't take much effort. You don't have to manufacture a compliment for every person that passes by. But by simply voicing the nice thoughts that go through all our heads on a daily basis—"I love your sweater," "What a beautiful smile," "You're so brave," "I'm so glad we're friends"—we can make the world a little bit better every day.

NOVEMBER 8

Challenge

Compliment someone on something you know they take pride in.

For Reflection

When was the last time someone complimented you on something you take pride in? What did they say, and how did you feel as a result?

How does it affect your confidence and improve your mood when someone recognizes something that matters to you?

What are some things your closest loved ones take pride in, and why?

How Did It Go?

Who did you compliment, and how did they respond?

NOVEMBER 9

Challenge

Compliment someone standing in a line with you, whether it's at a coffee shop, the post office, or the grocery store.

For Reflection

What do you usually do while waiting in lines in public places? Do you distract yourself to avoid connection?

What might be the benefit of connecting with a stranger in line?

Have you ever done this before, and if so, what was the result?

How Did It Go?

What compliment did you offer? Was this a gratifying experience? Why or why not?

NOVEMBER 10

Challenge

Give someone a small gift of appreciation for something they recently did for you.

Brainstorm: *For example, a bottle of wine, a box of candy, homemade cookies, or something smaller, like a cup of coffee.*

For Reflection

Has anyone done anything thoughtful or kind for you lately? If not, can you think of something someone did in the past that you never acknowledged?

Based on what you know about them, what small gift would they most enjoy, and why?

How Did It Go?

What gift did you give? Did the other person seem to appreciate this?

NOVEMBER 11

Challenge

Write down five compliments to yourself and read the list at every meal today.

1.

2.

3.

4.

5.

How Did It Go?

How do you feel about yourself at the end of the day after completing this exercise?

NOVEMBER 12

Challenge

Add a note of appreciation to the end of a work or personal e-mail. If you're feeling ambitious, add a note of appreciation to the end of *all* e-mails today.

Brainstorm: *You could thank a colleague for his work ethic or professionalism; you could thank a solicitor for sharing her product or service with you, even if you're not interested; you could thank a friend for always keeping his e-mails brief and to the point.*

For Reflection

Has anyone done this for you lately? If so, what did they acknowledge?

Was this something you would have recognized as praise-worthy? If not, how did it feel to receive praise for it regardless?

How might you make a difference in someone's day by offering unexpected praise?

How Did It Go?

Did you choose to do this for one e-mail or all? How did the person (or people) respond to your praise?

NOVEMBER 13

Challenge

Compliment a parent for doing their part to create a better world by raising their children well.

For Reflection

Who in your life is a parent who does a wonderful job with their children?

What do you admire about their parenting style?

How might the effects of their parenting ripple into the future, affecting the world at large?

How Did It Go?

Did you point out anything specific about this person's parenting style? Did they seem to appreciate this acknowledgment?

NOVEMBER 14

Challenge

Hang something in your home or workspace that reminds you to feel and express gratitude for the people in your life.

Brainstorm: *You could display an image with a quote about gratitude on your refrigerator, hang a framed blessing on your wall, or display a sticky note near your desk with the words "Who are you grateful for today?"*

For Reflection

Do you have a favorite quote about gratitude? How and why does this inspire you?

In what area of your life do you most need a boost of positive energy and reminder to focus on the good? At work? At home?

How Did It Go?

Did seeing this reminder throughout your day help you focus more on what you appreciate about the people in your life?

We became friends right away. We both had the same type of dog and walked them in our neighborhood, and we had both moved to the East Coast after living on the West Coast. We laughed a lot and shared our vulnerabilities with each other, looking for compassion and guidance. Even though our ages are ten years apart, it seemed we went through similar experiences.

After two years of sharing and doing so much together, we got into our first big fight. I was hurt that she did nothing for my fiftieth birthday, and let her know. She said she didn't think she could live up to my expectations and would have to think about if she could continue with our friendship.

That was it for me; that was the last straw. I stopped calling her, and she did the same. I felt I gave more to the relationship than she did and was tired of not getting much in return. As the months went on, I'd think about her every now and then, particularly when she had her second child, but I told myself it was a good thing to not be in touch with her because she would just continue to hurt me.

Almost an entire year went by until we ran into each other at an ice cream shop. We saw each other and she held out her arms to me. We hugged and picked up where we left off. As the weeks went on, we talked about our fight and what we both learned from it. She told me she learned she needed to share her feelings more, and I needed to appreciate what others give to me, not what they don't give. Appreciation—it seems so simple, but it changed everything for me. It took a big fight and a year of growing and healing, but I learned to appreciate all my friend has to offer, and it is plentiful.

Six hundred and twenty-three weeks ago on a Friday evening, I met my husband, Doug, for the first time after talking to each other on the Internet for a few months. We decided we would meet at a coffee shop, and if we clicked, Doug would make dinner for us that evening. If not, we would go our separate ways. Well, obviously that coffee date and dinner went well, as has every day since that significant night.

Every Friday since we met, we celebrate our love for each other with written letters. We thank each other for the life we have created together and the love that we share. We write about how much we appreciate all that we do for each other, promise to never take each other for granted, and recap all the memories from that week that we will treasure forever.

With the busy lives we lead, like everyone else, it is important for us to never lose sight of how much we matter to each other. We remember to focus on the little things, from opening the car door for each other, to kissing each other every morning when we wake up, as well as when we go our separate ways and before we fall asleep. For those nights when we are not together because of travel, we choose one of the greatest memories we have experienced together so that we can relive an adventure in our dreams.

We have had our difficulties—losing loved ones, open-heart surgery, and near-death experiences—and we deal with everyday challenges. But we have chosen to celebrate each other and every day we have together, and not to lose focus of what really matters. It is better to focus on kindness, thoughtfulness, and appreciation than all the little things that just don't matter at the end of the day.

NOVEMBER 15

Challenge

Appreciate what someone has done for you instead of complaining about what they haven't done—and (bonus!) tell them why you're grateful.

For Reflection

In which relationship do you frequently focus on what the other person hasn't done, or has done "wrong"?

What's something helpful or nice they've recently done for you, no matter how small, and how did this help you?

How might it improve your relationship if you focused more on these kinds of things?

How Did It Go?

Who did you appreciate, and for what? How do you think this affected them and your relationship?

NOVEMBER 16

Challenge

Whenever you talk to someone today, think of something you appreciate or admire about the person before speaking.

For Reflection

For which people in your life do you imagine this exercise will be challenging?

How might this change the way you see them?

How might this improve your interactions with these people?

How Did It Go?

Were you able to think of something you appreciate about everyone you spoke to today? Did this change how you engaged with them?

NOVEMBER 17

Challenge

Send someone a thank-you e-card for something that wouldn't ordinarily warrant a card—like their attention when you needed to vent, or the ride they gave you to work.

Tip: *Google "free e-cards" and you'll find a ton of options.*

For Reflection

Who in your life recently did something helpful or thoughtful?

How did this make your day easier or better?

How does this one act of consideration reflect the kind of person they are? What can you learn from them in this way?

How Did It Go?

Who did you send a thank-you card, and for what? Did they write back?

NOVEMBER 18

Challenge

Jot down any praise or compliments others offer you so you'll have a growing list of all the things others most appreciate about you.

For Reflection

What do you think your closest loved ones most appreciate about you, and why?

Are these also things you appreciate about yourself? If so, when was the last time you stopped to acknowledge yourself for these things?

How Did It Go?

Did you receive any compliments or praise today? Did you absorb these words more fully as a result of recording them to read later?

NOVEMBER 19

Challenge

Ask someone what they most appreciate about themselves to help them foster a deeper sense of self-gratitude. (If they demur, push them a little, showing the value of the exercise.)

For Reflection

Who in your life seems a little insecure or unsure of themselves?

How might they benefit from an invitation to reflect on their worth?

What do you see in them that you hope they see in themselves?

How Did It Go?

What did the other person share, and how do you think this exercise affected them?

NOVEMBER 20

Challenge

Invite someone in your life to be your gratitude partner—for the day, or for longer. E-mail them five things you're grateful for, and ask them to do the same.

For Reflection

Who in your life would most benefit from focusing on the good things in their life?

Do you think they'd be open to this? If not, how could you make this sound more appealing to them?

What things are you most grateful for today, and why?

How Did It Go?

Who did you invite to do this with you, and were they open to the idea? If so, what did they share with you?

NOVEMBER 21

Challenge

Tell someone the most important thing you've learned from him or her, and thank this person for that gift.

For Reflection

Who has taught you something that has helped you be the person you want to be, or live the life you want to live?

What specifically did they teach you, and how has this lesson helped you?

What do you think your life would be like if you had never learned this lesson?

How Did It Go?

Was this person surprised by what you shared? How do you think they felt knowing they made a difference for you in this way?

I can't help myself—I love sleeping with people. The more the better! There's nothing like crawling between the sheets with a lot of people. Female. Male. An armload of ethnicities. It's all good! Hey, don't look at me like I should be ashamed of myself, because I'm not! Besides, I know you do it, too. And you probably love it just as much as I do.

You think you know what I'm talking about, but I guarantee you're wrong. (Quick lesson: assumptions are not good!) See, what I mean is the thousands (yes, thousands) of people it takes to create the beds we sleep in. There are the people who extract the iron ore from the earth and the people who ship the ore to the mill workers, who separate the iron from the slag and then make the angle iron for the bed frame. There are the people who grow the cotton that will eventually be made into sheets and pillowcases. There are the people who make dyes, who in turn rely on the people who create the proper chemicals with petroleum or coal, which, of course, is the fruit of the labor of people who drill for oil or mine for coal. There are the loggers who cut the trees that will become headboards and footboards . . . I could go on and on and on!

And all those people represent only a few of the bed's components! The circle expands ever further. Consider the people who work to pay those people who make all the parts of your bed—not to mention those who work to harvest and produce the food consumed by all those individuals. And the people who build the vehicles to ship the parts . . . you get the picture!

And, of course, all these people would not be here if it wasn't for their parents, grandparents, great-grandparents, and so on. In the end, it is completely accurate to say billions of people sleep with you every night. We are all interconnected. The person who thinks of himself as completely independent is laughably mistaken. He eats food produced by fellow humans. He clothes himself with fabrics and materials made by fellow humans. When he is sick, he takes medicine produced by other humans or goes to other humans who will try to help him heal in doctor's offices and hospitals. He even depends on the animals and/or plants he eats for sustenance, and the rain that nourishes the plants, ad infinitum. There is no such thing as true independence.

Tonight, as you climb into your soft, comfortable bed, think about the fact that, in a very real sense, that bed is a gift to you from the whole world. Its story dates back to the birth of this planet—and beyond. It is truly amazing to ponder. Take a moment to be grateful for that gift, and then enjoy sleeping around, so to speak. Tell your friends to do it, too! If we all recognize our interconnectedness, it makes it that much harder to hate, and so much easier to appreciate all the ways we support and provide for each other.

NOVEMBER 22

Challenge

Think of something you use every day and can't imagine living without. Now write a short e-mail to the manufacturer thanking them for this, or leave a short note of appreciation on their Facebook page.

For Reflection

Why do you enjoy and appreciate this item so much?

What do you want the manufacturer to know about their contribution to the world?

Have you ever done something like this before? If not, why?

How Did It Go?

What did you write, and how do you think this affected the manufacturer or its employees for the better?

NOVEMBER 23

Challenge

Replace a critical thought about someone with a grateful thought.

Brainstorm: *If your friend shows up late to dinner and you think,* She's never on time. Our relationship must not be that important, *you could replace that with* I'm grateful that she makes time for our friendship, even if she often runs late.

For Reflection

Who do you most often criticize, out loud or in your head, and what does this accomplish?

What was the last critical thing you thought about someone, and (for practice) what grateful thought could you have replaced it with?

Is there anyone in your life you wish would do this for you? How might that improve your relationship?

How Did It Go?

Which critical thought did you replace? How did this affect your feelings about the other person, and consequently, your interaction?

NOVEMBER 24

Challenge

Write a short thank-you note to leave in
your mailbox for your mail carrier.

For Reflection

What's something you've taken for granted about the mail and service you receive?

Why is this something worth appreciating?

How often do you think mail carriers get thanked for their service?

How Did It Go?

How did you feel after doing this? Did your mail carrier acknowledge this in any way?

NOVEMBER 25

Challenge

Leave a short, anonymous note of appreciation in a public place where someone who needs it might find it. For example, it could read: "You make the world a better place, and we thank you for it."

Brainstorm: *You could leave this on a mirror in a public restroom or on a corkboard where people leave business cards and promotional materials in a coffee shop.*

For Reflection

What message of gratitude would you appreciate seeing in a public place?

Why would this particular message be meaningful or valuable to you?

What might the world be like if everyone took this message to heart?

How Did It Go?

What message did you write, and did you see anyone's response to it? Do you think this affected them in a positive way?

NOVEMBER 26

Challenge

Identify someone who provided you with excellent customer service, and write a short letter to their manager praising their efforts.

For Reflection

In what way did this person go above and beyond?

How did this impact your experience, and why did you appreciate it?

How might it benefit this person to reach out to their manager with a few words of praise?

How Did It Go?

What did you write, and did the person's manager write back?

NOVEMBER 27

Challenge

Write a letter to your younger self, thanking him or her for any wise decisions that led you to where you are today. If you're not pleased with where your decisions have led you, thank your younger self for being brave enough to take chances, even if they didn't pan out as you'd hoped they would.

Dear younger self,

How Did It Go?

How did you feel about yourself and your life after writing this?

NOVEMBER 28

Challenge

Go for a short walk with the intention of complimenting three people you see, whether they're neighbors, passersby, or people working.

For Reflection

What do you think makes a good compliment?

Have you ever felt that a compliment from a stranger held more weight, since there was no ulterior motive—positive or negative—behind it?

How might a short walk focused on gratitude actually be an act of kindness to yourself?

How Did It Go?

What compliments did you offer, and how did people respond? How did you feel after your walk?

NOVEMBER 29

Challenge

Before a meal today, thank everyone whose efforts brought that food to your table, from the farmers to the distributors to the grocery store employees.

For Reflection

Do you usually offer words of appreciation before meals? If so, do you feel gratitude when doing this, or do you do it without really thinking about the words?

Does it make you feel more grateful and connected to others to recognize how we all impact one another's lives?

How Did It Go?

Did you feel appreciation when doing this? Did you enjoy your meal more as a result?

NOVEMBER 30

Challenge

Thank a loved one for something you usually take for granted.

For Reflection

Why do you think you take this for granted, and how do you think your loved one feels about this?

Why is this something worth acknowledging? How does it help you or make a difference in your life?

What do you think your loved one will most appreciate about your words of gratitude?

How Did It Go?

What did you acknowledge, and what did your loved one say in response?

MONTHLY REVIEW

- Which challenges were the most helpful for you, and why?
- Which challenges were the most difficult for you, and why?
- What did you learn about yourself through the process of completing these challenges? Did you form any new insights about admiration and appreciation?
- What did you learn about the people in your life?
- Did these challenges strengthen your relationships, and how?
- Did you identify any areas for improvement and growth?
- Head over to http://tinybuddha.com/love-forums to share your experiences with other readers!

DECEMBER

Giving and Receiving

Reflections from BJ BURMAN

Adam is a friend of mine. At best, you might call him careful with money. At worst, and probably closer to the truth, you'd say he was, well, stingy. Sorry, Adam! Adam said he grew up poor, and money certainly was tight. His parents were always scrambling to pay the bills—much like many of us these days! He grew up thinking that there "wasn't enough for everyone" and that he had to "get what he could for himself." Don't get me wrong—Adam is a lovely guy, but he was scared and acted from that.

The thing is, this attitude of hoarding that Adam lived by meant that not only did he not spend or give away his money, but he also became stingy with his time and love. Friends would ask him to go on holiday with them, and he'd say no because he wouldn't want to spend the money. His best friend needed some financial help, but Adam said no because he couldn't bring himself to part with the money. He ended up parting with his friend instead. For Adam, it might have initially been about withholding money, but it ended with him withholding himself, his love, and his life.

About a year ago, Adam was in a horrendous car accident. He could easily have died, but he walked away with only minor injuries. Acutely aware that it could have gone the other way, this changed him completely. He suddenly had firsthand experience of how fragile life is, and how short it can be. After the accident, he started spending money. Not crazily, but generously. He spent money on having great experiences with his friends and people he loved. He started to participate more in life. He started to open up and give more of himself. He also started donating money to charities. That blew our minds!

Even his relationship with his partner improved. She had been on the verge of leaving him because he would not let her into his life and his heart in an open way. After the accident, it was like they fell in love all over again. (Surprise! That girlfriend is me!) But what I notice most is that while the old Adam never smiled much, and always seemed slightly worried about something, the new Adam seems to smile all the time, or if he isn't happy, we at least know how he is feeling, because he gives himself by letting us in.

And Adam will tell you, ever since the accident, people came out of nowhere to help him, in a way that never happened before. Adam says that because he was now a giving person, the world seemed to want to give to him as well.

I sincerely hope that we don't have to experience a life-threatening situation to realize the incredible joy of giving to others, and of receiving what others give to us. I hope that instead of coming from a position of lack, of believing there's not enough for everyone, we understand the paradoxical miracle of giving—that whatever we give to others, we will, in some way, receive back in abundance. It's not an easy habit to break, I know—we are conditioned to think this way. But we need to claim a happier life. A life of giving freely and receiving gratefully. At the very least, giving feels good! That alone is reason enough to give.

DECEMBER 1

Challenge

Give your greatest gift to someone else today.

Brainstorm: *If your compassion is your greatest gift, be a shoulder for someone to lean on; if your knack for organizing is your greatest gift, help someone declutter their desk or room; if your creative talent is your greatest gift, make something to give someone else.*

For Reflection

How has this gift served you in the past?

Have you used this gift to help others before? If so, how do you think this made a difference in their lives?

How would you most enjoy giving this gift to someone today? What might they appreciate about this?

How Did It Go?

How did you give your gift? How do you think this made a difference in the recipient's day?

DECEMBER 2

Challenge

Give a friend, coworker, or loved one their favorite item or experience today.

Brainstorm: *You could bring them their favorite snack or magazine, let them play their favorite song in the car, or invite them to do their favorite activity, your treat.*

For Reflection

Why does your friend, coworker, or loved one enjoy this item or activity?

How does it affect their mood when they get to enjoy this?

Why might they appreciate this gesture on this day specifically?

How Did It Go?

What favorite item or activity did you provide? Did it lift their spirits?

DECEMBER 3

Challenge

Give an acquaintance your phone number or e-mail address so that you can connect on a deeper level sometime in the future.

For Reflection

Who in your life would you like to get to know a little better, and why?

What's prevented you from connecting on a deeper level up until now?

What do you have in common that you could share to help get the ball rolling?

How Did It Go?

Did you feel nervous or awkward doing this? Are you glad you did?

DECEMBER 4

Challenge

Pay someone a compliment on something you believe they're insecure about to help boost their confidence.

For Reflection

Who in your life could benefit from a little reassurance, and why?

How have they been hard on themselves, and how has this affected their life?

How have they made progress in the area where they feel insecure?

How Did It Go?

What compliment did you give, and did they willingly accept it? How do you think you made a difference in their day?

DECEMBER 5

Challenge

Give yourself a break. Schedule a little time into your day to simply be.

Brainstorm: *You could take a nap or a bath, or sit in nature.*

For Reflection

In what way have you felt most stressed lately? Mentally? Physically? Emotionally?

What would be most beneficial for your well-being, and why?

How might it affect your day if you prioritized this?

How Did It Go?

What did you choose to do, and how did you feel as a result?

DECEMBER 6

Challenge

Set aside a jar that you can fill with loose change and eventually donate to a cause or charity that you care about.

For Reflection

What's one cause that means a lot to you? Why do you feel passionate about this cause?

How might your donation help others who are struggling, perhaps in the same way as you once did?

Putting coins into a jar doesn't always feel like a big display of generosity at the time, but how do you think this small act helps grow a generous spirit?

How Did It Go?

Did you already contribute to the jar? How did this simple act affect your state of mind?

DECEMBER 7

Challenge

Give your time to someone today, whether that means lending an ear, a hand, or a shoulder.

For Reflection

Do you regularly give your time to people? Why or why not?

What do you think you convey to others when you give them your time?

Why might time be more valuable than other gifts you can give?

How Did It Go?

What did you decide to give? Did the other person willingly accept it? How do you think this was helpful to them?

When I was committed to loving myself more, I started to become aware of how I treated myself and realized that I did not know how to receive. There were times when I would squirm and act awkward when I was given extra attention. Other times I'd feel indebted when I received a big gift or if someone did me a huge favor. Then, there were others when I'd feel like I was imposing when a person offered to do something for me.

I remember a time when I was around fifteen years old. I went to my friend's house to play cards. Around dinnertime, my friend's mom invited me to stay to eat with them. I politely turned her down, telling her I'd be going home soon anyway. She insisted, and I insisted on refusing to accept the invitation. I appreciated her offer, but I didn't want to impose, so I felt it was more polite to decline.

Later that night, my friend said her mom thought it was strange of me to keep turning her down. I was shocked and hurt. I didn't accept the invitation because I didn't want to hassle her into having to prepare for an additional dinner plate. I had no intention of offending her. It was only recently that I truly understood what happened. I denied her the chance to give. I also robbed both of us the chance to connect. I was so focused on not wanting to impose that I forgot to just be grateful for her offer.

If we refuse to receive, it will leave us empty and even resentful. And it can be harmful to relationships, because we're not able to recognize and appreciate everything the other person has to offer. We should always be focused on giving, but we should also learn to accept blessings gratefully. Once the door to receiving is open, imagine how many gifts are waiting for us.

I wish I could say that I'm a graceful receiver, but that's not entirely true. I appreciate being thought of, but I'm often uncomfortable when standing on the receiving end of things. Yet, if anyone were to ask me if both giving and receiving were necessary components for healthy relationships, I would, without a second thought, say yes.

Early on, we are programmed that it's "better to give than to receive." The depiction of those who give is one of virtuous and upright character, while little emphasis, if any, is placed on the receiver. With such admiration and almost martyrdom placed on givers, it's understandable why learning how to properly receive can be difficult.

In no other experience has my struggle with receiving been as apparent as with my new boyfriend. He's amazing. He sees that I am a giver and wants to give to me. Of his time. Of his resources. Of his mind. But to receive it means that I actually have to be vulnerable. I have to open up. Beyond my past, beyond my fears, and beyond all the reasons why I should "know better" than to let him in. It would be so easy for me to reject him, to say, "I've done it on my own till now—I'm good." Each time he shares something with me, it's a lesson in receiving to not thwart his efforts with a well-intentioned but ill-placed "no, thank you."

For far too long I've worn my inability to receive like a badge of honor, as though being in the deficit physically and emotionally is a position to be admired. I now realize my unwillingness to receive not only compromises my relationships, but it compromises me. I've decided to remain in this vulnerable but necessary place, knowing that it is the only way I can truly grow. I'm eons ahead in the giving game, and it's about time the receiver in me caught up.

DECEMBER 8

Challenge

Make "I am worthy" your mantra today, and think this whenever someone offers you anything, whether it's their seat on the bus, their attention, or their support.

For Reflection

Do you believe that you are worthy of receiving—and why or why not?

What's one reason a loved one might offer as proof that you are, in fact, worthy?

What would you say if *you* were the loved one speaking to someone else in your shoes?

How Did It Go?

What did you receive today? Did this mantra affect your thoughts about those gifts and accepting them?

DECEMBER 9

Challenge

Ask someone directly for what you want instead of hinting at it or giving to them in the hopes of inviting reciprocity.

For Reflection

In which relationship do you sometimes struggle to communicate what you want?

What do you fear will happen if you're clear and direct?

Is it better to be in a relationship in which you stay quiet and frustrated? How do you think this will affect the relationship down the line?

How Did It Go?

What did you ask for today, and how did it feel to be direct? Was the other person able to meet your request?

DECEMBER 10

Challenge

Identify a relationship in which you give more than you receive, and then ask that person to be there for you in some way today, whether that means lending an ear or offering their greatest skill to help you.

For Reflection

What have you given in this relationship, and what have you wanted that you haven't received?

What have you gained by maintaining a relationship with this kind of imbalance—even if just the knowledge that you're a "good person" for being so giving?

How might it benefit both of you to shift the balance a little?

How Did It Go?

What did you ask for, and how did the other person respond? Do you think this strengthened your relationship?

DECEMBER 11

Challenge

Ask someone to assist with a task you've been dreading, both to help you finish more quickly and to make it more enjoyable.

For Reflection

Why have you been dreading this task?

Why might this be easier or even fun if you ask someone else to help you with this?

How could you make this task less daunting and more enjoyable for the two of you?

How Did It Go?

Who did you ask, and did you already work on this task together? If so, what did you most appreciate about having help?

DECEMBER 12

Challenge

Accept all compliments today with "Thank you" and a smile instead of brushing off your accomplishments or feeling a need to appear humble.

For Reflection

How do you usually feel when someone gives you a compliment, and how do you respond?

When you give someone a compliment, what is your intention? Does this change your perspective on how you respond to compliments?

How would you respond to compliments if you considered each one a gift that the giver wants to see you enjoy?

How Did It Go?

Did you receive any compliments today? How did it feel to accept these with a smile? How do you think the other person (or people) felt to see your gracious reaction?

DECEMBER 13

Challenge

Share this quote from Amanda Owen, author of *The Power of Receiving*, with any friends who try to "do it all" and then wonder why they don't get back what they give: *"The only possible match for someone who doesn't know how to receive is someone who doesn't know how to give."*

For Reflection

Who in your life tries to do it all, and what does "all" entail for them?

How does this affect them and their relationships?

How might it change their life if they truly internalized this idea—and acted on it?

How Did It Go?

Who did you share this quote with? Do you think it was helpful for them to gain a new perspective on their giving nature?

DECEMBER 14

Challenge

Write down a few things you believe your best friend deserves from her relationships. Now identify in which of your own relationships you're settling for less and why, and choose one need you'll assert today instead of settling.

Brainstorm: *For example, needs could be time, attention, unconditional acceptance, or commitment.*

What your friend deserves:

In which relationship(s) you're settling for less, and why:

What need you'll assert today:

How Did It Go?

Was this exercise eye-opening for you? What need did you decide to assert, and how do you feel about doing this?

I had just withdrawn funds at the bank and then moved down the counter to organize my paperwork. The woman behind me stepped up to the teller and presented a withdrawal slip. The teller refused her request for cash, saying her account was overdrawn. The woman let out a cry, and several customers turned to see where it came from. Her voice was breaking as she wailed, "What am I going to do!"

Without thinking, I did something I never do. Now, I must tell you that I don't give even small change to people sitting on the sidewalks holding out their hands or hats. I donate occasional modest sums to a few of my favorite spiritual organizations. That's it. But hearing the woman, I reached into my cash envelope, took a step closer to her, and held out a hundred-dollar bill. She looked at me, unbelieving. I smiled and extended the bill closer to her. Her eyes tearing, she took it.

My act didn't have any direct or immediate consequences like those we read about. I didn't receive a check for quadruple that amount in the mail, a sudden gift of something expensive I'd longed for, or a registered letter of an inheritance from an unknown relative. But what I gained from my action was much more important. I never missed the money and felt certain that it met the woman's urgent immediate need. We never even exchanged names, but I still cherish her look when I held out the bill, as if the heavens opened. Her face glowed and she hugged me. "Bless you!" I imagine her thriving and remind myself that I suffered no loss.

This experience taught me that whatever we are moved to give—whether it's money, a smile, a hand, a suggestion, or a few minutes of undivided attention—we should. Yes, the receiver gains what is needed. But as givers, we too gain incalculably from our spontaneous acts of giving from the heart.

It was Amma's (my mother's) birthday, the third one since her passing. I always missed her on the day. When we lived in India, I would be on the phone first thing in the morning, wishing her a happy birthday and singing for her. Later in the day, my daughter and I would visit her with gifts. Together, we'd eat cake or some homemade delicacy she'd dish up. The day was about celebration, joy, and connection.

After her transition, it was a day of empty hours. Now there was nothing to do. No one to celebrate. Or . . . was there? How would Amma make this day special? What would she have done? Almost as if she were listening and waiting for me to ask, the answer dropped into my head. The doom and gloom of moments ago vanished. My mood shifted. All of a sudden I was energized.

I drove to the senior living community where I facilitated a weekly Story Group. Walking up to the front desk, I said hello to Cindy, the receptionist whose sweet spirit and gentle manner reminded me of Amma. I pulled out a tiny pouch from my bag and handed it to her.

"What's this, Uma?" she asked, curious and expectant.

"Open it."

She tugged the strings apart and out spilled a pair of jade-green earrings and a matching bead necklace.

"It's beautiful, but . . . it's not my birthday," said Cindy, looking a tad confused.

"I know. It's my mother's birthday and she's been gone three years. I'd love to celebrate you today. This is her jewelry. I think she'd like you to have it."

Cindy's eyes misted over, as did mine. When a loved one crosses over, the love doesn't die. We just find a different way to express and experience the connection, and for me, that was giving Cindy the jewelry. Love is what Amma was, and what she continues to be. I knew she was smiling over this moment between Cindy and me, a very happy birthday girl.

DECEMBER 15

Challenge

Offer a friend who is struggling financially something of yours (that's in good condition) that you're planning to replace soon.

For Reflection

Has anyone ever done anything like this for you?

If so, how did this help you?

Would it ever have occurred to you to ask someone for something you knew they didn't need anymore? If not, why?

How Did It Go?

Was the person excited to receive this item from you? How do you think it will make a difference in their life?

DECEMBER 16

Challenge

Share something you enjoy with someone in your life.

Brainstorm: *Invite someone over to share that bottle of wine you've been saving, pack your favorite meal for lunch and bring extra for a coworker, or buy yourself a dozen roses and give half to a friend or roommate.*

For Reflection

Which of your favorite treats do you most enjoy sharing with others, and why?

What do you gain in sharing a treat with someone as opposed to keeping it for yourself?

Why would you appreciate it if someone invited you to share something they love?

How Did It Go?

What treat did you share, and with whom? Did they appreciate this? What did you enjoy most about the experience?

DECEMBER 17

Challenge

Think about the greatest gift you've ever received. Write below who gave it to you, what it was, why this was meaningful to you, and what you learned from the experience. Now utilize this lesson to give a meaningful gift to someone else.

Brainstorm: *This could be a gift for the holiday season, a birthday gift that you give sometime down the road, or a "just because" gift to show someone you care.*

The greatest gift you've ever received:

Who gave it to you:

Why this was meaningful to you:

What you learned from this experience:

How Did It Go?

What gift did you decide to give? Are you excited about giving it, and why?

DECEMBER 18

Challenge

Give a friend in need a book that helped you, and write a personal inscription to them on the cover page.

For Reflection

What's one book (that you still have in your possession) that has made a tremendous difference in your life?

In what way was this book helpful or meaningful to you?

Who in your life could benefit from reading this, and why?

How Did It Go?

What did you say when you gave your friend the book? How did your friend respond?

DECEMBER 19

Challenge

Give yourself a push—do something that you know is good for you, but you sometimes struggle to do. (Really, it's a gift to yourself!)

Brainstorm: *This could be something for your body, like jogging; something for your mind, like unplugging from technology and reading a book instead; or something for your spirit, like meditating.*

For Reflection

Why do you have such a hard time doing this thing?

Why do you want to do this, in spite of the difficulty? What benefits do you receive when you do it?

How can you make this easier or more fun so that you can motivate yourself to do this today—even if just for a short while?

How Did It Go?

What did you do, and how did you feel after doing it?

DECEMBER 20

Challenge

Give something to someone who you think doesn't need it, to practice giving without judgment and to reinforce that we are all worthy of receiving.

For Reflection

Why do you believe this person does not need or deserve assistance?

What's one reason this may not be true?

Why might they appreciate this gesture, whether they need the gift or not?

How Did It Go?

What did you give, and was this hard for you? How did the other person respond?

DECEMBER 21

Challenge

Do something to give back to your community.

Brainstorm: *You could take canned goods to a food drive, give a homeless person something they may need, like a toothbrush and toothpaste or a clean pair of socks, or pick up litter in your neighborhood.*

For Reflection

Who do you know who has done a lot for their community, and what can you learn from them?

Do you regularly give back to your community? If so, how, and if not, why not?

What type of giving would you find most personally rewarding, and why?

How Did It Go?

How did you decide to give back? How do you think this act of generosity made a difference?

When my father was diagnosed with colon cancer, I had no idea that four years later I'd be caring for him during his last weeks of life. I never asked "Why me?," but I did question my ability to help him.

When we were told that there was nothing more that could be done, I brought him home with me. I wanted to care for him until his last breath. By this time he could hardly walk, eat, or drink. Within days after coming home, he stopped walking altogether and became bed-bound.

My dad constantly apologized to me for being such an inconvenience, a bother. Each time I'd reassure him that all I wanted was for him to be comfortable. It didn't matter, though, for up until he uttered his last words, he apologized for everything I had to do for him.

At that point he required around-the-clock care. His wounds needed constant changing of dressing. He needed to be moved to his sides throughout the day to avoid getting bedsores. He needed to be sponge-bathed and given water with a dropper, as he could no longer swallow. And when he began to gasp for air, unable to speak, he needed someone to stay by his side to administer meds to help him breathe.

On the surface, it seemed as if I gave a lot. After all, caring for my dad became a full-time job. But caring for my dad during the last days of his life gave me the opportunity to cultivate and practice compassion, tolerance, understanding, unconditional love, and increase my capacity for pain. Nothing, absolutely nothing I gave him could possibly compare to what I received from him.

When we focus only on what we give, we risk not seeing what we receive. We must pay close attention and look beyond the surface so we don't miss it, for often what is given to us is something incredibly valuable to our personal evolution.

A few years ago, my husband and I bought a fixer-upper home from the 1950s and spent two tough seasons fixing it up. When we finally finished, we were tired, relieved, and proud. We decided to have a housewarming party to celebrate our achievement and to show off all our hard work. I printed out invitations to give to our new neighbors and e-mailed friends in the area to invite them. One friend responded, "I'd love to come, but I don't think I'll be able to make the trip from Chicago to D.C."

I was confused. Everyone I'd invited lived in the D.C. area. I looked more closely at the response and realized I'd accidentally invited an old high school friend. She had the same first name as a current friend, and my e-mail service had auto-completed the e-mail address with the wrong last name without my realizing it. I e-mailed her back, explaining my gaffe, and noted that I hadn't expected her to make a cross-country flight for our housewarming.

Our party came and went. Everyone oohed and aahed at the transformation our home had gone through. And then a few days later a box of flowers arrived at our doorstep. They were from my high school friend. She'd sent them with a note, congratulating us on our new home. I was so touched by her kindness. We hadn't been in contact for several years, but she'd still seen fit to send us a housewarming gift after an accidental e-mail.

This friend taught me that it's always appropriate to celebrate the milestone achievements of the people in our lives, no matter how close we are. After all, it's not every day that we finish a big project, get married, have a baby, or win an award. An act of thoughtfulness can make someone's day, the way the flowers my high school friend sent me made mine.

DECEMBER 22

Challenge

Give a friend credit for an accomplishment or milestone, whether verbally or in writing, with an e-mail, letter, or card.

For Reflection

Has anyone done this for you lately? If so, what did you most appreciate about this?

Why is your friend's accomplishment or milestone more impressive or important than they may realize?

Why do you think it's important to acknowledge our friends' milestones and accomplishments?

How Did It Go?

How did you choose to acknowledge this accomplishment or milestone? How did your friend respond?

DECEMBER 23

Challenge

Give yourself some credit. Make a list of at least three things you've done right recently and write for each one reason that it's something to be proud of.

Brainstorm: *You can be proud of yourself for devoting a half hour to looking for a new job because it would have been easier to zone out in front of the TV after work; you can be proud of yourself for replacing one can of soda with a glass of water because it's hard to break a caffeine habit, and a small change is better than none at all.*

1. What you did right:

   Why this is something to be proud of:

2. What you did right:

   Why this is something to be proud of:

3. What you did right:

   Why this is something to be proud of:

How Did It Go?

How did it feel to recognize and give yourself credit for these things?

DECEMBER 24

Challenge

Say no today instead of agreeing to do something that will deplete your energy or require you to sacrifice something you need to give to yourself.

For Reflection

For which reasons have you said yes when you've wanted to say no in the past?

How has this negatively affected you and your relationships?

What's something you can say to kindly but firmly decline requests so you don't compromise your needs today?

How Did It Go?

To whom did you say no, and how did it feel to do this? Did this enable you to better take care of yourself?

DECEMBER 25

Challenge

Receive all criticism with gratitude today, looking for some lesson within it—even if the only lesson is to have a thicker skin and take things less personally.

For Reflection

How do you usually respond to criticism?

How does it affect you and your relationships when you respond in this way?

Does it change how you feel about criticism—and the people who deliver it—to consider there's always something valuable within it?

How Did It Go?

Did you receive any criticism today? Were you able to receive it with gratitude? Did you recognize anything you could work on in the future?

DECEMBER 26

Challenge

Do something for someone else that could be considered an inconvenience, and identify one thing you receive from being there for them in this way, even if it's simply an opportunity to practice acceptance.

Brainstorm: *For example, through completing a task for your coworker, you could receive an opportunity to improve at that task; through doing a chore for your roommate, you could receive a chance to do something physical and get out of your head.*

For Reflection

Have you ever received an unexpected benefit from doing something for someone else?

What did you give, and what did you receive?

How did this gain help you or enrich your life?

How Did It Go?

What did you do, and what did you receive? Was it helpful to shift your perspective in this way?

DECEMBER 27

Challenge

Make a small donation on kickstarter.com, gofundme.com, or another fund-raising site, or donate to a third world entrepreneur on kiva.com. (Even a few dollars counts!)

For Reflection

Do you know anyone who's raising money for a project or goal?

If not, what type of project or cause would you most like to support?

How do you often feel about donating money in this way? Do you find it a valuable use of your money? Why or why not?

How Did It Go?

What project did you support, and what excites you about this?

DECEMBER 28

Challenge

Think of three recent experiences when you asked for something and were rejected. Write below what you asked for, why it was hard to ask, and why you shouldn't let this discourage you from asking someone else for this in the future. Refer to this whenever you feel nervous to ask for something you want or need.

Brainstorm: *For example, asking someone out on a date, asking someone for help, asking someone to donate to your cause, or asking someone to promote your work*

1. What you asked for:

   Why it was hard to ask:

   Why you shouldn't let this discourage you:

2. What you asked for:

   Why it was hard to ask:

   Why you shouldn't let this discourage you:

3. What you asked for:

   Why it was hard to ask:

   Why you shouldn't let this discourage you:

How Did It Go?

Did this exercise help you view rejections differently? Do you feel better able to continue asking for what you want and need?

DECEMBER 29

Challenge

Give yourself permission to splurge a little.

Brainstorm: *You could eat your favorite meal out, treat yourself to a massage, or if money is tight, buy something more affordable, like your favorite coffee drink.*

For Reflection

When was the last time you splurged on yourself, and what did you most enjoy about this?

Do you feel guilty when you spend money on yourself? Why or why not?

If money is tight right now, is there anything you can cut back on this week to allow yourself this splurge?

How Did It Go?

How did you splurge on yourself, and how did you feel as a result?

DECEMBER 30

Challenge

Whenever you feel tempted to complain about something you're not getting today, do something proactive to address your need instead.

Brainstorm: *If you're tempted to complain about someone who doesn't give you their attention, ask them if they'd turn off their phone over dinner; if you're tempted to complain about someone who doesn't give you the same support you give them, ask them to help you with something specific.*

For Reflection

What type of things do you often complain about not receiving?

What usually happens as a result of complaining, and does it solve anything?

What's something proactive you could do to meet this need?

How Did It Go?

Were you tempted to complain in this way today? If so, how did you proactively meet your need? How did this help you, and do you think it strengthened your relationship?

DECEMBER 31

Challenge

If these challenges have improved your relationships or enriched your life, give someone else the link to check out this book (http://tinybuddha.com/love-book)—or (bonus!) give them a copy as a gift.

For Reflection

How has using this book improved your relationships and enriched your life?

Who do you know who could benefit from these challenges?

MONTHLY REVIEW

- Which challenges were the most helpful for you, and why?
- Which challenges were the most difficult for you, and why?
- What did you learn about yourself through the process of completing these challenges? Did you form any new insights about giving and receiving?
- What did you learn about the people in your life?
- Did these challenges strengthen your relationships, and how?
- Did you identify any areas for improvement and growth?
- Head over to http://tinybuddha.com/love-forums to share your experiences with other readers!

Contributors

Alan Eisenberg

Alan Eisenberg is an e-learning expert by day and an antibullying activist at night, helping people recover from long-term bullying issues. Since 2007 he has published web support through www.bullyinglte.wordpress.com.

Alana Mbanza

Alana Mbanza is a freelance writer and author of *Love Sick: Learning to Love and Let Go*. Visit her at www.alanambanza.com to learn more about her coaching and freelance writing services.

Alison Elissa Cardy

Alison Elissa Cardy is a professional career direction coach who specializes in helping people get unstuck and onto satisfying career paths. Her website is www.alisonelissa.com.

Alyssa Deis

Alyssa Deis is a girl with a type-A personality who aspires to make the world a better place. She loves morning coffee and tries to live a simpler life.

Ameena Payne

A soul learning to follow its Divine Path, Ameena is passionate about encouraging mindful living and social responsibility. Visit her at www.ameenapayne.com.

Amy Connors

Amy Connors is a lawyer turned yoga teacher and mother of three young children. She believes it's her greatest mission in life to help others lead a more compassionate life. Visit her at www.theyogacrusher.com.

Amy Johnson, Ph.D.

Dr. Amy Johnson is a psychologist, life coach, and the author of several books, including *Being Human: Essays on Thoughtmares, Bouncing Back,* and *Your True Nature*. Visit her at www.DrAmyJohnson.com.

Andrea Still

Andrea will teach you how to feel calm around other people while feeling comfortable within yourself. To find out more, go to: www.hangoutwithoutfreakingout.com.

Anne Bechard

Anne Bechard is on a mission to prove that you can totally follow your passion and keep your career. She founded www.bloggerswithdayjobs.com to turn nine-to-fivers into bloggers with a life.

Anne Gillme

Anne founded Expatriate Connection (www.expatriateconnection.com), an online community to address what's missing in expatriates' lives: how to deal with loneliness, expat grief, loss of identity, and uprooted children.

Ashley Rankin

Ashley Rankin is an inspirational freelance writer whose popular post on the Chinese Bamboo is featured on PaulCBrunson.com. For more inspiration, visit http://ashleyrankin.wix.com/writer. Tweet her @anikole21.

Bill Lee

Bill Lee is a former gang member, recovering addict, and retired headhunter. The author of three memoirs, his latest book is titled *Born-Again Buddhist*. Visit his author page at http://amzn.to/14k6wYM.

BJ Burman

Author BJ Burman helps people overcome the grief of loss using the philosophy of karma. In a world where we so desperately seek happiness, karma is key. Visit http://www.karmalifelove.com.

Bree Barton

Bree has published stories in *PANK*, op-eds in *USA Today* and the *L.A. Times*, and essays in *McSweeney's*. She teaches dance and loves Brussels sprouts. Catch up with her at www.breebarton.com.

Charlotte Wirth

Charlotte Wirth is from Luxembourg and has studied at the University of St. Andrews. She has a passion for horses and used to work for an international eventing rider in Germany.

Claire De Boer

Claire De Boer is a writer and teacher with a passion for stories and a strong belief in their power to connect and heal us. Find her at www.thegiftofwriting.com.

Cloris Kylie

Cloris Kylie is a performance coach and personal branding expert who helps you make a living doing what you love. Find her programs, articles, and complementary resources at www.cloriskylie.com.

Corie Weaver

Corie Weaver is a writer and artist who has recently started a publishing house for quality middle grade and young adult science fiction and fantasy stories. Visit www.StudioWeaver.com for more.

Cynthia McFayden

Cynthia McFayden just celebrated her tenth wedding anniversary. The blessings and challenges that life offers are a reminder of how precious life is and the ones we share it with.

David Munger

David Munger is a software user-interface designer living and working in the Chicago area. A longtime fan of inspirational literature, David writes about these topics in his blog at www.inneryonder.com.

Deborah Shelby

Deborah is a voracious reader, full-time working mom of teenagers, and writer.

Denise Dare

Denise Dare is a Happiness Artist on a mission to inspire visionaries to live their dreams and enjoy the journey. Join the Happiness Revolution: http://denisedare.com.

Ehren Prudhel

To read more from Ehren Prudhel, please visit his website at www.ehrenprudhel.com.

Elaine Martini

Elaine is an architect, worktop designer, writer, jewelry maker, traveler, explorer, and student. She is learning, appreciating beauty, and trying to become a better person each day. Visit www.elainemartini.com, follow @nanemartini or see her jewelry at www.triouz.etsy.com.

Ellen Bard

Ellen Bard is a psychologist and business consultant—and global traveler, self-improvement crusader, and heroine of her own adventure story. Visit http://ellenbard.com/tiny-buddha for insightful articles and resources on personal development.

Emma Letessier

Emma Letessier is the editor of *Barefoot Vegan*, a digital magazine that promotes veganism, spirituality, and living in close connection with nature. You can subscribe for free at www.barefootvegan.com.

Ernest Dempsey

Ernest Dempsey is a counselor, a blogger, and a fiction and personal development author. You can check out his inspiring blog, helpful books, and thrilling novels at ernestdempsey.net.

Gigi Griffis

Gigi Griffis is a world-traveling writer with a special love for living in the moment. Find her adventures, her musings, her traveling pooch, and her unconventional travel guides at www.gigigriffis.com.

Grace Furman

Grace Furman is on a lifelong endeavor to live mindfully and heartfully. She blogs about ethical and ecofriendly living, health, nutrition, and more at www.heartfulhabits.com.

Haiku Kwon

Haiku Kwon's journey has led her to a place where learning to trust is also teaching her to love and be loved. Read more at www.haikukwon.com.

Hannah Braime

Hannah Braime is a coach who helps people create a life on the outside that reflects who they are on the inside. You can find her at:
www.becomingwhoyouare.net.

Heather Day

Heather Day is a Costa Rica–based lifestyle consultant and yoga teacher who has made it her sacred mission to provide women with the tools to leap bravely toward their dreams. Website: www.heatherdaywellness.com.

Heather Holly

Heather Holly has her M.A. in clinical psychology and works in the mental health industry. She has been a burgeoning writer and artist since she learned how to hold a pen.

Jamie Jo Hoang

Author of *Blue Sun, Yellow Sky*. Writer. Thinker. Explorer. Lover of tea. Never far from an ocean. Website: www.heyjamie.com. Twitter: @heyjamie.

Janice Li Pascual

Janice Li Pascual is striving to live a meaningful life. She combines two loves: cartoons and personal development to create Mind Snapshots (www.mindsnapshots.com). Web Comics for the soul.

Jayati Ghose

Jayati lives to write and can be usually found behind a book. She is the creative head at www.freemindtraining.com/blog. For a good cappuccino she will tell you a story.

Jennifer Boyer-Switala

Jennifer Boyer-Switala is a wife, mom, history teacher, writer, and photographer. She is also an enthusiastic (some say obsessive) Francophile who blogs about all things French at http://leblog1815.blogspot.com.

Jessica Latham

Jessica Latham's writing and philosophy stems from daring to live with passion, authenticity, and love. Find more of her work on www.jessicalatham.com or www.rowdyprisoners.com.

Jill Dahl

Jill Dahl is the founder of Secondhand Therapy (www.secondhandtherapy.com). She is on a mission to help busy women move beyond survival mode and start investing in their emotional well-being.

Julia Rymut
Julia Rymut continues having grand adventures and lots of love. She helps you do the same with the art of walking, playing, and writing. You can find her at www.TaraTrue.com.

Julian Hall
Julian started Calm People because he wanted businesses to profit from taking more care of their employees' emotional well-being because emotionally resilient employees are more efficient. Visit him at www.calmpeople.com.

Karina Kainth
Karina Kainth uses her background in international policy/education to lead heart-centered youth programs. She believes that intercultural understanding leads to a more enlightened world. Connect with her here: www.linkedin.com/pub/karina-kainth/56/734/242/.

Ken Wert
Ken Wert is the founder of www.meanttobehappy.com where he writes about happiness and living a life of character, courage, clarity, passion, and purpose.

Laura G. Jones
Laura G. Jones helps creative grasshoppers design flexible productivity systems that honor their natural rhythms. Learn how to conquer burnout, being overwhelmed, and procrastination without suffocating schedules at www.lauragjones.com.

Lauren Stewart
Lauren Stewart is currently working as a marketing/event coordinator for a nonprofit in Michigan and freelance writes for a beauty and health website. She resides in Michigan. Visit her at www.laurenrstewart.weebly.com.

Lily Velez
Lily Velez is a speaker and author who teaches people how to live more fulfilling lives. To discover what's holding you back from the life of your dreams, visit www.lilyvelez.com.

Linda Carvalho
Linda would like to thank her husband and family for their ongoing support. Her inspiration is attributed to the students and people she has worked with throughout her teaching career.

Louise Crooks

Louise Crooks a.k.a. The Keys to Clarity! Coach has a vision of supporting coaches, healers, and transformation catalysts to grow their businesses, so more people are helped and healed. Visit www.keystoclarity.com.

Louise Jensen

Louise Jensen is a mindfulness meditation coach, specializing in anxiety, depression, and chronic pain. She established a practice to cope with her disability and has completed extensive teacher training programs. Visit www.thehappystarfish.co.uk.

Marissa Walter

Marissa Walter is a trainee counselor and writer of Break Up and Shine, a website to inspire and support healing after the end of a relationship. Visit her at www.breakupandshine.com.

Melissa Lopez

Melissa Lopez is a writer and a visual artist. She is passionate about helping people build their confidence and stamp out their self-limiting beliefs. You can visit her at www.boldstepsforabiglife.com.

Megna Murali

Megna is an amateur writer who finds solace in the written word. She likes to put one word after the other and watch magic happen. Read more on www.thoughtsthatmakemetick.wordpress.com.

Michelle Faust-Davis

Michelle Faust-Davis is a therapist who lives in Arizona with her husband and three cats. She enjoys traveling, playing the keyboard, and flying the trapeze. You can find her at www.felinesofphoenix.blogspot.com.

Michelle Russell

Michelle Russell blogs at www.enoughist.com, where she helps people cut through life's overwhelmingness and figure out what it means to *have* enough, *do* enough, and *be* enough.

Noelle Sterne

Author and dissertation coach Noelle Sterne, Ph.D., combines practicality and spirituality in *Challenges in Writing Your Dissertation* (forthcoming). Noelle's book *Trust Your Life* (Unity Books) helps readers reach lifelong yearnings. Visit www.trustyourlifenow.com.

Pat Roa-Perez

Pat Roa-Perez, writer, is committed to raising awareness on the plight and prevalence of mental illness, access to quality care, and stopping the cycle of depression in families. Visit www.reinventedwomenonly.com.

Paul Sanders

Paul Sanders (www.getthefriendsyouwant.com) teaches people how to: overcome shyness and loneliness, master conversation and social skills, and make friends and build a social circle.

Peter Fernando

Peter Fernando trained as a Buddhist monk in the Thai Forest tradition for seven years. Upon leaving the monastic life he has been teaching online and in Wellington, New Zealand, since 2009. Visit www.monthofmindfulness.info.

Rebekah Moan

Rebekah Moan is a writer, editor, blogger, and inspirational speaker. Her book, *Just a Girl from Kansas,* is available now. To read the insights she learns every week, visit her blog www.anotherworldisprobable.com.

Reshma Patel

Reshma Patel is a doctor of physical therapy turned true healer. She loves to write/blog and is inspired by life and her two beautiful daughters. Visit www.endlesspossibilities.org and www.endlesshealing.org.

Sara Avery

Sara Avery helps people remove their biggest roadblocks in relationships, health, career, and self-expression. Learn how you can experience the unprecedented changes her clients rave about at www.quantachange.com.

Sara O.

Sara O. lives in Massachusetts. She enjoys being around dogs, helping others, and practicing self-love.

Skylor Powell

Skylor Powell is a wellness author and yoga instructor. Visit her at www.skylorpowell.com.

Stacey Lance

Stacey Lance loves to inspire others through writing, public speaking, and performing. Her passions include nature, animals, and music. You can find her at www.soulspiral.blogspot.com and on twitter @staceylance13.

Stephanie Hauck

Stephanie Hauck is a teacher by profession, a lover of music, and an avid traveler. She aspires to have a life filled with love, laughter, and adventure.

Summer Star Howard

Summer lives with her deliciously blended family near Boulder, Colorado. Find her articles, videos, and free relationship and intuitive coaching at www.summerhoward.com. Go ahead . . . follow Summer to relationship bliss!

Trish Murphy

Trish Murphy is the owner of Mentoring by Trish. She mentors children who need support and behavior modification. Her passion is helping children build self-confidence and self-awareness. Visit her at www.mentoringbytrish.com.

Uma Girish

Uma Girish is a grief guide, dream coach, and Hay House author. Her transformational memoir is *Losing Amma, Finding Home: A Memoir About Love, Loss and Life's Detours*. Visit www.umagirish.com and www.internationalgriefcouncil.org.

Vironika Tugaleva

Vironika Tugaleva is an inspirational speaker, life coach, and award-winning author of *The Love Mindset*. She helps people develop self-awareness, self-love, and peace of mind. Reach her at www.vironika.org.

Wilfried Lehmkuhler

Wilfried Lehmkuhler is a life and performance coach who has worked with professional athletes all over the world. He's the founder of www.financialfreedomandalifeyoulove.com, creating personal success strategically.

Acknowledgments

After writing thirty different ways to show admiration and appreciation, a few lines of thanks seems insufficient, but I'd like to briefly acknowledge a few extraordinary individuals, nonetheless.

First and foremost, thank you to the contributors who shared their experiences, insights, and lessons. I appreciate that you're part of the Tiny Buddha community, and I'm grateful that I had the privilege of including your stories in this book.

To the people whose efforts sustain tinybuddha.com—Joshua Denney of Think Web Strategy, the team at Press Labs, and the many other contributors whose stories may appear in future books—thank you for helping so many, myself included, feel less alone with their struggles and more empowered to overcome them.

To my agent, Linda Konner, thank you for your expertise and support, and for helping me find the best possible home for this project. You are truly exceptional at what you do, and I feel fortunate to have connected with you.

To Karen Salmansohn, thank you for your guidance, encouragement, and general awesomeness. I'm so inspired by your work, and grateful for the opportunity to learn from you.

To Katy Hamilton, editor extraordinaire, this was truly a collaborative experience, and I was blown away by the time, effort, and care you put into this project. Thank you for helping me go deeper, get more creative, and shape this book into what I hoped it would be.

And to the people I love, from coast to coast, thank you for being you, and for loving me.